VASTU LIVING

KATHLEEN COX

Illustrations by Allison Eden Karn

VASTU
LIVING

Creating A Home
For The Soul

Marlowe & Company
New York

Published by
Marlowe & Company
841 Broadway, 4th Floor
New York, NY 10003

Vastu Living: *Creating a Home for the Soul*
Copyright © 2000 by Kathleen Cox
Illustrations copyright © 2000 by Allison Eden Karn
Preface copyright © 2000 by Swami Sada Shiva Tirtha

Grateful acknowledgment is made to Sudesh Prabhakar for permission to reprint "Ode to the Universe" on page 91.

Library of Congress Cataloging-in-Publication Data

Cox, Kathleen M., 1939-
      Vastu living : creating a home for the soul / by Kathleen Cox.
        p. cm.
      ISBN 1-56924-644-0
      1. Vastu.   2. Hindu astrology.   3. Architecture, Hindu.   I. Title.

  BF1779.V38 C69 2000
  133.3—dc21

                                                                                00-020153

9 8 7 6 5 4 3 2

BOOK DESIGN BY PAULINE NEUWIRTH, NEUWIRTH & ASSOCIATES, INC.

Printed in the United States of America
Distributed by Publishers Group West

For Sudesh Prabhakar
a great architect, scholar, and friend

Contents

PREFACE   XI

ACKNOWLEDGMENTS   XIII

LIST OF ILLUSTRATIONS   XV

TO THE READER   XIX

INTRODUCTION   1

PART ONE THE JOURNEY   15

1   THE *VEDAS* AND VASTU   17

CONTENTS

2   THE VASTU PURUSHA MANDALA   37

3   VASTU IN ANCIENT TEMPLE DESIGN   57

4   VASTU AND THE VEDIC VIEW OF HEALTH   79

PART TWO   CREATING A HOME FOR THE SOUL   93

5   GETTING STARTED   97
    Determining Your Needs and Preferences   97
    Expressing Your Self   101
    Creating Your Spiritual Blueprints   102

6   VASTU LIVING AT HOME   111
    The Vastu Home   111
    Orientation and Shape   117
    Interior Layout   121
    Room by Room   125
    Putting the Divine in the Décor   149

7   VASTU LIVING AT WORK   154
    Spirituality at Work   154
    Orientation and Shape   157
    Interior Layout   160
    Room by Room   165

8   THE GIFT OF NATURE   177
    Landscape and Outdoor Gardens   178
    Celebrating Nature Indoors   186

CONTENTS

9 APPEASING THE GODS—APPEASING YOUR SOUL   193

Examples of Common Problems   194

The Solutions   195

APPENDIX I: THE RAGA AND VASTU   217

APPENDIX II: HARMONY THROUGH DIET   223

GLOSSARY   230

BIBLIOGRAPHY   234

QUICK REFERENCE CHART   237

VASTU PURUSHA MANDALAS   240

ABOUT THE AUTHOR AND THE ILLUSTRATOR   247

PREFACE

DIFFERENT PARTS OF the Hindu Vedas—a collection of writings that first appeared in India more than 5,000 years ago—describe universal laws of nature as they pertain to all fields of life. For instance, the world's first science of health, ayurveda, is first articulated in the Vedas, as is its sister science, yoga. Yoga, of course, has been practiced in North America for many years now, and in the past decade ayurveda has become quite well known, as well.

Vastu shastra, an equally ancient Vedic science related to architecture and interior design, explains the universal laws of nature as they pertain to built structures and the environment. While ayurveda treats the health of people, vastu treats the health of structures; vastu is ayurveda for buildings. The sciences of ayurveda and vastu are quite intertwined; like morning glory vines on a wooden fence, they are wrapped around each other and together make a more beautiful and serene vista.

Where shall I begin with the praises due this book? *Vastu Living* breaks new ground in many ways: It is the first book on vastu to offer an easy, hands-on method of bringing natural beauty, balance, and serenity to your home, apartment, office, or other structure. This is also the first vastu book to utilize ayurveda as a practical method of molding your personal vastu living and working spaces.

Vastu Living offers something for everyone—history, culture, science, spirituality, healing, and everything you need to fully implement vastu into your life, including do-it-yourself floor plans. Moreover, Kathleen Cox sets the record straight as to the true dignity and contribution India has made in so many fields of life—from mathematics to music, and she dispels many of the myths about Hinduism that, surprisingly, exist even to this day.

And let me tell you: *Vastu Living* works. Following its advice, my colleagues and I re-arranged some of the furniture in our ayurveda center. We changed the seating arrangement in order to face east when working on the computer. We created a "zone of tranquility" and moved the tall, heavy furniture out of the northeast. We also placed one of our rugs in the sacred space. We felt positive changes in the clinic immediately, changes that transformed our workplace into an even more peaceful and productive space.

Vastu Living teaches you how to create heaven on earth in your own home and office. I highly recommend this book to all people looking for more health, peace, and serenity in their lives.

—SWAMI SADA SHIVA TIRTHA, D.SC.,
author of *The Ayurveda Encyclopedia*
and director of the Ayurveda Holistic Center
and School of Ayurvedic Science in Bayville, New York

ACKNOWLEDGMENTS

WHEN I FIRST visited India in 1985, I had no idea that this country would have such an impact on my life and my future. Over the years, I have been enriched by irreplaceable friends, who showered me with their kindness and warmth. These same friends, during the course of my study of vastu, opened new doors in India that led to friendships with extraordinary people working in the fields of vastu, architecture, archaeology, ayurveda, music, and yoga. So many people helped me on my vastu journey.

I thank my dear friends from India, who are truly family to me—Toshi and B.K. Goswami, Ranu and Pradip Prasad and their daughters Bhavna and

xiii

Divya, and Usha Bhanot—for their unending support and hospitality. Other generous friends also willingly opened doors for me: Vivek Srivastava, Kiran Sachdev, Nishat Mummunka, and Shubra Gupta. I also want to thank Professor H.D. Chhaya for his patience and guidance, Sudesh Prabhakar for his willingness to share his knowledge about the Vedic culture, vastu and architecture with me, Dr. Pandit Vishwanath Sharma and his son Anurag whose remarkable family started Shree Baidyanath Ayurved Bhawan, India's oldest ayurveda company. Finally, I would like to thank Suneet Paul (editor of India's finest architecture and design magazine, *A+D*), Parveen Chopra (editor and publisher of India's New Age magazine, *Life Positive*), and Krishna Deva, India's brilliant archeologist and the author of *Khajuraho*.

After I returned from India to Manhattan, numerous friends in the United States also offered their support and excellent advice throughout the months of preparation of this manuscript. They were all invaluable allies—my daughter Kia, Kathryn Kilgore, Larry Estridge, Reniera Wolff, Chris Lupton, Sally Helgesen, Laura Rittenhouse, Tannia and Manu Goswami. I also want to thank four very special people for their enthusiasm and contribution: my illustrator, Allison Eden Karn; my agent, Kathy Anderson; and my editors, Matthew Lore and Caroline Pincus.

xiv

LIST OF ILLUSTRATIONS

Symbol of AUM	26
Tala System	31
Vastu Purusha Mandala	38
Vedic Altar	41
Vedic Illustration of the Human Form	42
Da Vinci's *Vitruvian Man*	42
Marma Points and Diagonals on the Vastu Purusha Mandala	44
Diagram of the Deities for 81 Squares	46
Rotation of the Earth Around the Sun	48
Vastu Purusha Mandala with Elements and Cardinal Deities	53

Hindu Trinity Family Tree   60

Brahma   61

Saraswati   61

Shiva   61

Parvati   62

Durga   62

Ganesha   62

Vishnu   62

Lakshmi   63

Rama   63

Krishna   63

Hanuman   63

Linga and Yoni   65

Diagram of the Zones   67

Exterior of the Kandariya Mahadeva   69

Diagram of Temple Interior   73

Diagram of Quadrants for a Rectangle Oriented East and West   103

Diagram of Quadrants for a Rectangle Oriented North and South   103

Diagram of an L-Shaped Home or Property   104

Diagram of the "Quirky" Site   105

Small Zone of Tranquility   114

Mahatma Gandhi   116

Vastu Kitchen Layout   125

Vastu Dining Room Layout   129

Vastu Living Room Layout   131

Indian Swing   133

Vastu Home Office or Study Layout   135

Vastu Zone of Tranquility Layout   138

Vastu Master Bedroom Layout   143

Vastu Children's Bedroom Layout   145

Indian Toran   152

Vastu Reception Area Layout   165

Vastu Conference Room Layout   166

Vastu Office Layout   169
Vastu Cubicle Layout   172
Vastu Garden Diagram   185
Vastu Terrace Garden   191
Brahma   200
Saraswati   202
Shiva   203
Parvati   205
Durga   205
Ganesha   206
Vishnu   207
Lakshmi   209
Rama   210
Krishna   211
Hanuman   212

To the Reader

Vastu Living: Creating a Home for the Soul offers an introduction to the ancient Indian way of vastu, a system for organizing the spaces in which we live and work for optimum harmony. In this age of high-speed technology, which has radically altered our lifestyle, we have been the beneficiary of many new products and services; but we all know that these benefits come with a price. Ever-changing choices, along with conflicting obligations at home and at work, are making many of us feel tense and stressed. We are pressed for invaluable time that we need to share with our family or with others, and for personal time that allows us to go deep within our intimate self. Precious time has gone the way of the rotary phone, and we have lost sight of who we are and what we really need in order to achieve a healthy sense of well-being and fulfillment.

Vastu, an ancient and wise spiritual science that, like yoga and ayurveda, originated in the subcontinent's Vedic culture, can be an important ally in our wired new world. Vastu believes that how we align our physical space in relation to nature and how we set up the interiors inside a structure have a powerful impact on us—an impact that can be either positive or negative. Vastu creates personal spaces that let us unwind and feel at home so that once again we can hear our inner voice that speaks softly, gently, yet honestly to us. If we follow vastu and create a home and workplace that reflects the perfect balance that exists in the universe, we will rediscover our connection to everything that exists around us and, by extension, we will rediscover our inner voice, our inner guide.

And what is vastu? Hindus modestly call it their science of architecture. It is not just about aesthetics but about the nature of the universe and our connection and relationship to it. Specifically, vastu is based on the Vedic idea that harmony within and without come from observing our proper relationship with every space we inhabit. In other words, before we can achieve internal peace, we need to find external peace. To this end, vastu helps us rediscover a life of balance and well-being by creating a healthy and soothing environment in our home and in our workspace.

How do we achieve this balance? We achieve it through vastu's amalgamation of science and spirituality. We show respect for all creation and honor the ancient concept of the five basic elements of space, air, fire, water, and earth. If we keep them in harmony, we, in turn, achieve a harmonious relationship with them that brings us peace. We also accept the truth of the all-encompassing divinity that extends from a pebble to every organism that shares our shrinking world. This includes the divinity of our own true self.

Acquiring respect for the self. Think about it. It's strange that all of us have so eagerly embraced the appropriateness of ecology and holism—their essential goodness. But the truth is that most of us don't really understand the meaning of these two words. If we did, why haven't we completely embraced these concepts and applied them to that critical part of us—our own self? If we believe in the holistic "oneness" that exists in everything around us, then why don't we extend this belief to our "oneness" with everything else—and protect our self from harm as well?

This is the heart and impetus behind *Vastu Living: Creating a Home for the Soul.*

PART ONE

Part One of *Vastu Living* explains some key concepts in the Vedic philosophy. Hinduism, vastu, yoga, and its ancillary practice of meditation, ayurveda (the science of life and the earliest form of health care to focus on disease prevention)—all of these disciplines are branches that stretch out from the same tree. They originated in the Vedic texts and are founded on a meaningful fusion of science and spirituality. Vastu even shares similarities with ragas, which are more than exquisite musical compositions that adhere to a mathematical structure. Ragas are spiritual and act as a therapy for the soul.

Readers familiar with these disciplines will realize that it is this fusion of science and spirituality that makes the experience of each discipline feel so inherently right. The entire body and mind receive a carefully reasoned workout or work-over with yoga and ayurveda; and with all these disciplines, the unseen soul feels nurtured and calm. This is true with all Vedic sciences. They exhibit a sophisticated logic and understanding that is comingled with spiritual beliefs that are uplifting and liberating.

Vastu Living comes from the knowledge that I acquired from writing about India since 1985 and from living in New Delhi for nearly nine years. I was guided in my study of vastu by a special mentor, and the practice of vastu is fully integrated into my life. I know vastu's power, how it has changed the way I think about myself and my relationship to everything else in the world.

XXI

PART TWO

To prepare *Vastu Living* for a Western audience, I have adapted the science so that it will work in a culture and environment that are so very different from India. I discussed these adaptations with my mentor and he was receptive and encouraging. My goal was always to remain faithful to the tradition while bringing you as close to the essence of vastu as possible. Certain of the customary objects that have long been incorporated into the Indian home, for example, require a new adaptation for the West. Differences in climate and terrain also dictate certain modifications. Such changes are unavoidable, since the world is made up of diverse habitats, climates, and societies. Consider the birds that share our planet—the extraordinary assortment of nests that they create to meet the needs of different conditions in diverse habitats. This is true with all life forms.

One of the most significant differences between my approach and the Indian one is that in India, vastu is connected to astrology or *jyotish*. Jyotish is an integral part of life for many Hindus: astrological charts are often compared, for example, to determine if a marriage will even take place. Dates of many important events are frequently determined by jyotish. Nehru postponed the birth of India as a free democratic country by one day because too many Hindus believed that the original date of August 14 was inauspicious.

Jyotish, a serious adjunct to astronomy, is extremely complex and quite different from Western astrology. It takes years to learn and depends on knowing one's exact time and place of birth. No approximations. Unfortunately, few of us know the actual minute of our birth. This information is not even included on many birth certificates. Instead of using jyotish or Western astrology with vastu, I use a personality-typing system that incorporates aspects of ayurveda, vastu's sister science. This accomplishes the same objective, namely to determine an alignment and use of space that is appropriate for you.

I suggest that you curl up on a bed or in an easy chair and read this book carefully. The ancient theories that are expressed in Part One reveal deep wisdom. You may be tempted to skip ahead to the practice, but I urge you not to do that. Without the background, you will almost certainly not get the full benefits of vastu. When you read Part Two and learn how to incorporate vastu in your own life, use the same care. If you do, there is a good chance that vastu will work for you as it does for me. In your home, you will discover a harmony within yourself and a feeling of ease with the ones who may be living with you. In your workspace, you will find a sense of balance where you feel connected with your work. And over time these new feelings will become the prevailing part of your interior self and change, forever, how you relate to the environment from the smallest to the largest definition of that word.

But please remember that neither vastu nor this book promises a dramatic overnight change. Vastu living is not a quick fix. Like feng shui, this ancient Hindu practice requires more than a new fish bowl or the pleasant sound of wind chimes. It can take some tinkering before your spaces are properly tuned. Just think of it as zeroing in on a station on an old-fashioned radio. Turning that dial until it finally gets rid of the static can take a while. This is how it works with vastu living. It requires an honest careful study of yourself and your surroundings.

Vastu also asks you to gaze intently at the world around you. Consider, too, the rest of the world that is so far away from your window that you can't even describe it. Take into account the wonder of all that is in the universe, including the wonder that exists inside you. Can you see that everything is interconnected and interrelated, and that all existence benefits from a state of mutual harmony and balance? Can you see how this concept logically extends to our physical space? If you can say yes or want to say yes, then draw upon the wisdom of vastu. This spiritual science can create a gentle home for your soul and the souls of the ones you love who share your space.

INTRODUCTION

I strive hard to preserve my physical body.
Do I take the same pains to know my soul?

MAHATMA GANDHI[1]

THE WORD *VASTU*, a mysterious word delivered with the reverence of a mystic *mantra*, or chanted sacred formula, was first uttered to me in 1995 when I was living in New Delhi. I remember the day. I had gone to visit a close Indian friend and her family, which was part of my weekly routine. I entered her beautiful house and headed toward her lounge when I realized that most of the furniture and many of the Indian artifacts had been shifted around and the function of many rooms had completely changed. The living room had become the dining room. The daughter's

[1] M.K. Gandhi, *A Thought for the Day*, Ananad T. Hingorani, trans. (New Delhi: Publications Division, Ministry of Information and Broadcasting, Government of India, Fourth ed., 1994).

1

bedroom had become the master bedroom. The former master bedroom now belonged to a son; and the daughter took over her brother's bedroom.

"What's going on?" I asked.

"Vastu," said my friend. "It's an ancient Hindu science. It creates harmony in the house." She looked at me with her coy smile. "Come, have tea." She led me into the lounge, one of the few rooms that had retained its former identity.

Vastu. Yet another puzzling Hindu concept to file in my mind. I discovered soon after I first went to India in 1985 that no matter how much I learned about the Hindu culture, there was always something important that I still needed to know. Hinduism is as multifaceted as the Koh-i-noor diamond.

Some of my friends have a *puja* (prayer) room. In the early morning the room fills with the delicate odor of incense and the sound of clanging bells as the family priest or a family member chants Sanskrit prayers and rotates a flame from burning oil, which acknowledges the sacred deity in the small shrine as a symbol of the light of truth. Fresh petals float in a bowl of rose-water and delicate sweets on a tiny silver dish are offered up to the god or goddess who is so carefully enshrined.

Just as many friends, however, never perform a daily puja in the home. But their personal behavior still reflects their faith, such as the traditional *namaste* greeting with palms together and fingers held upright in front of the heart—a blessing that honors the divine that resides within the soul. Ritual actions are in evidence throughout the day, and are so ingrained that Hindus perform them spontaneously.

For two years I continued to meet people at New Delhi parties and events who had done their home "as per vastu"—the popular phrase of the initiated. Or they'd done their luxurious "getaway" farmhouse just outside the capital or a fancy old British bungalow, rented flat, factory, or office.

During these same two years, I got a peek at the theories behind this science by listening to what people had to say about vastu. Vastu, it seemed, went way beyond design, form, utility, durability—concepts that define architecture. It rose up from a base that molded together spirituality and ancient scientific views that continue to withstand the test of time. In fact, in recent decades many Western scientists engaged in the world of quantum physics have begun to look with interest into Eastern philosophy and its views about the creation of the cosmos. Some of them believe that their own new theories are just catching up with the old.[2]

Vastu, a mixture of strong spiritual philosophy and science, revolves around the belief that everything in the universe is interconnected and interdependent. Therefore, it is important to maintain the order and balance that is inherent in the universe. To do this, vastu looks carefully at the orientation of physical space so that it reinforces the ancient theories connected to the five primary elements: space, air, fire, water, and earth, which are present in our environment and within each of us. Vastu offers guidelines—not hard and fast rules—that help us choose the best alignment and use of a space so it will reinforce our own well-being.

Vastu also honors the specific deities that are related to each one of these elements and to the cardinal directions. When we respect the domain of each element and its deity and when we respect the deities connected to the individual cardinal directions, we respect the natural order of the universe. Surya, for example, is the sun god, who lords over the east and enlightenment. We cannot live without the presence of the sun. We also improve our life through spiritual wisdom and knowledge. Yama, the lord of death and *dharma* (or duty), lords over the south. Death, of course, comes to all life; paying attention to duty reminds us to live responsibly.

The ultimate objective in vastu is to put harmony and order into any built space occupied by the human body. An orderly and harmonious space leads to an orderly and harmonious inner life, which is so necessary for the good health of the body, mind, and soul—and by extension, of everything that exists around us.

By allowing for the harmonious balance of the five basic elements, a building designed in accordance with vastu principles permits the positive vibra-

---

[2] See Fritjof Capra, *The Tao of Physics—An exploration of the parallels between modern physics and Eastern mysticism* (Boston: Shambala, 1991).

tions that flow through the universe to be properly channeled throughout the vastu space. A successful vastu home also encourages optimum vibrations to thrive and flow within the individual. The proper flow of these positive vibrations allows for the discovery or rediscovery of inner peace. Conversely, vastu blocks out the negative energies induced by negative forces.

In a vastu room, a deliberate decision to leave the center area empty of furniture creates an "airiness." This center space symbolizes the realm of Brahma, the supreme Hindu god of creation, and His central zone collects spiritual energy that then radiates out in every direction. An open center in a bedroom is not always possible; but even in these rooms, the idea is to keep the decor uncluttered.

People who swear by the power of vastu make incredible claims. Once vastu is factored into their space, they say, a newly found inner peace improves their concentration and allows them to make thoughtful decisions within the personal realm or in the world of business. Stress and tension decrease. They function better, their health improves—and many even claim that they find financial success. Most everyone insists that vastu simply makes good sense. It is logical. It is related, not just to the five elements, but to the sun, the moon, everything in the universe. It is scientific *and* spiritual.

I heard variants of these phrases from everyone. But no one who practiced vastu was ever able to explain the intricate levels of the science to me. The information that I gathered was just the froth that skimmed the surface of a subject that I knew had to run extremely deep.

I confess that initially much of what I heard about vastu, especially the claims about health and wealth, brought out the cynic in me. I was even amused that converts traveled with a compass to make certain that a temporary home or office on the road could be adjusted as per vastu in order to retain inner tranquility. Indeed, the compass was right up there with the passport, tickets, and credit cards on the "don't forget" list. Part of me even dismissed vastu as a form of superstition akin to touching wood in order to ward away bad luck—a popular and instinctive gesture made by many of my friends.

Initially, I also found all this room swapping and room reorganization disorienting—a funny thought since orientation is an integral part of vastu. Time and again, I proved the adage that old habits die hard. Often I opened the wrong door in a friend's house to find myself in the newly designated servants' quarters or a kid's playroom. But over time, I slowly realized that the changes within each room from the decor to the arrangement of the furniture almost always made me feel good. A vastu space put me at ease.

It was clear that a room's new character affected me on some deep level, where it didn't matter if I liked the Victorian-style chairs or Euro-style sofa (I prefer traditional Indian decor). When I sat on a chair or a cushion and just gazed around a once familiar space, I slowly filtered in the changes in little details. A carved deity now faced a different direction or had been removed to a new location in another room. New plants that were often imbued with spiritual meaning were now arranged in the room and seemed perfectly right, as if they grew there.

IN LATE 1997, my time in India was unexpectedly cut short. A serious personal matter rushed me back to New York City. When I returned to Manhattan, I discovered that feng shui, the Chinese art of placement, had become wildly popular. This ancient theory of design, which evolved from Taoism and Buddhism around the sixth century BC, seemed vaguely related to vastu. But no one had heard of vastu, which a few Indian authorities date back to 5000 BC or earlier (exact dates are not known). What made this seem so remarkable was that yoga had been popular in the States for so many years. And *ayurveda*—the Hindu science of life introduced through the works of Deepak Chopra and others—was also making its mark. Doctors and hospitals were even picking up on it, and companies were flooding the American market with "new" ayurveda-based remedies. Ashrams and retreats, ayurveda clinics, yoga and meditation centers—clearly Americans were interested in things Indian. At the very least, I thought, these folks would be interested to know that they could be enhancing the benefits of all these other Hindu disciplines by practicing them in a setting that followed vastu guidelines.

During the next few months, I thought repeatedly about vastu's ability to provide inner peace, tranquility, and a positive connection to one's place. The pace of city life felt far too fast. I felt as if I had lost control over my time and my life. Everyone I knew complained about the conflicting demands that pulled at them every day: demands at work, demands at home.

I began to think about the possible value of vastu in the West. Maybe we, too, needed to make a home for the soul, or *atma*, as it is called in Hinduism. Maybe if we considered the needs of the soul in our home or workspace, we would have a shot at inner peace. This sacred part of *me* certainly needed some nurturing and attention. I was not doing well in New York City.

All these thoughts reshaped into one phrase: *learn about vastu*. Learn how to turn a soulless space into a sacred place so that we in the West could achieve the positive results that everyone raved about in New Delhi. I visited the great libraries of New York City, but they offered little illumination on vastu. I failed to find any English versions of the ancient texts on this science that I knew had been translated over the years.

To succeed in my mission, I realized that I had to return to New Delhi. This city was so dear to my heart that I was also certain my own healing process would conclude while I was there. So a little more than a year after I had landed in New York City, I packed my bags and returned to my adopted homeland of India.

I WAS AMAZED to find upon my return that vastu's resurgence had really picked up speed, at least in the northern and central parts of India. Throughout most of southern India, vastu has always been an active part of the culture. I'd never noticed its presence because New Delhi was my former base as a journalist. And, while I traveled extensively, people in the south never mentioned vastu to me. It was so assimilated into their lives that they didn't think it required an explanation. It would be like a Westerner explaining the use of silverware at a meal; it's just a part of life.

But everywhere I looked in New Delhi I saw evidence of vastu. Huge real-estate advertisements in newspapers announced residential complexes and townships, and BASED ON VASTU was printed in bold, capital letters. The

Times of India, the country's most important English daily, featured an advice column on vastu that addressed readers' queries from how to save a failing sugar mill to how to get rid of the guest that won't leave.

Vastu experts were so confident that, in many New Delhi neighborhoods, they would show up uninvited at someone's front door, and they were usually invited inside. One friend told me how two consultants arrived on the same day, fortunately not at the same time. I watched "Home Style," a popular television show that ran on the local New Delhi government channel, where a swami, with long flowing hair and beard, was now the vastu guru.

The Apollo Hospital Group, which is revolutionizing the standards of medical care in India with its chain of attractive private hospitals, incorporates vastu into the design. The Apollo in New Delhi started functioning in 1996; it broke even six months later. Some Apollo hospitals are now planned for Arab countries. Indeed, many vastu consultants now included Middle Eastern Arabs and Asians from the Far East among their clients.

An article in the *Economic Times*, the sister newspaper of the *Times of India*, reported that a finance company was offering forty-year-term home loans at competitive rates to individuals who constructed their residences according to vastu. The company was also offering a free vastu consulting service. According to the article, the company's managing director claimed that the application of vastu in the design of a house dramatically cut the risk of loan default since vastu creates an environment for financial success. The company also assumed that the forty-year term loans would be repaid quickly— in a fast seven to nine years. Many people said that they thought that all these vastu-designed homes would be a great improvement over the dreary government constructions that were built in New Delhi and other Indian cities after the country's independence in 1947.

Most New Delhi bookstores had a section dedicated to new books on vastu; but the majority of these publications focused on "instant" wealth, health, and fame. The power of fear had replaced the promise of greater spiritual well-being, and there was scant reference to science. But this boom in vastu books also extended to the availability of the English translations of some of the great Sanskrit texts on the Hindu science that had been discovered in different regions of this huge country. Of particular interest to me were the eight-volume *Manasara Series* and the two-volume set of *Mayamata*, two of the best historic codifications of vastu.

I immediately enrolled in yoga and meditation classes, determined to get to know the ancient disciplines related to vastu. I spoke with top executives at Shree Baidyanath Ayurved Bhawan, the oldest company producing ayurveda products in India, about this great science that promotes well-being and disease prevention. I sat in on my friend Toshi's singing classes and listened as she and her sister Usha worked hard to learn the parts of a *raga* (Indian classical music). Their concentration was intense as they struggled to locate the precise vocal melody and control of breath. To ignore or violate the mathematical structure that is built into this intricate system of music (and classical Indian dance) breaches the harmony.

Harmony. Controlled flow of breath. Proper alignment. The Hindu sciences are so interconnected that they share a common vocabulary and emphasis. And vastu seemed to be in the center of it all. After all, what's the point in trying to improve the body and mind if the surrounding environment fails to reinforce these objectives?

I met more vastu believers with a personal story to tell. One young woman admitted that a consultant, on the first visit to her house, figured out that her marriage was in trouble. The consultant said that she and her husband should move from the house where they were living. Once she and her husband moved into their new house, which was vastu-designed, the friction between them subsided and all seemed well.

Sanjay Bindal, the managing director and owner of Modern Industries, heard about vastu in 1989. His fiancé's uncle in Hydrabad had built his entire factory as per vastu. The result? No business problems whatsoever. Bindal, a vastu skeptic, barely listened to the story. In fact, he couldn't add any further details.

But then, near the end of 1994, Bindal's company, which manufactures railway cars and other products in its factory outside New Delhi, was on the brink of the industrial "sick" list. Business had slowed down. Labor problems turned ludicrous. "Some workers refused to follow a schedule of hours. I mean after lunch some of them just disappeared for the day." Bindal laughed.

Bindal reconsidered his rejection of vastu. He called in a vastu consultant who made corrective changes. By 1996, positive results had improved the company's health. The difficult laborers disappeared for good. Orders flowed in. Visitors who sat in Bindal's office volunteered that the room made them feel comfortable.

Vastu led to such success for Bindal and his company that it motivated him to embrace many of the other Hindu sciences. He hired a yoga expert, who runs a daily yoga program for all the employees. This has also increased productivity and efficiency. Now the company plans to pipe classical Indian music throughout the premises: morning ragas that give mental peace and concentration; afternoon ragas that energize; and evening ragas that are restful.

In between my classes and meetings with vastu practitioners, I was also determined to find my own vastu teacher who would be willing to share his knowledge with me. I knew there were a lot of quacks trying to make a bundle of bucks off vastu, and from what I'd been hearing, in their hands it had all gotten rather misconstrued. I was looking for someone who was familiar with some of the ancient vastu texts and had a genuine foundation in its science and architecture.

I arranged meetings with scholars and archaeologists. After many meetings, one scholar put me in touch with a man who, he felt, could lead me to the perfect teacher. I made an appointment with the gentleman and early the next afternoon I set off in a three-wheeled motorized rickshaw into the sultry heat of New Delhi. After puttering up and down dusty narrow streets in a modest neighborhood, the driver finally located the basement office of Professor H.D. Chhaya.

This respected professor, who teaches at New Delhi's prestigious School of Planning and Architecture, sat behind a metal desk that had neither a computer nor a typewriter. An empty chair was positioned in front of his desk as if awaiting a visitor. A metal file cabinet was tucked in one corner of the humble basement. About fifty books were crammed into a wood bookcase against a distant wall far from the professor's desk. There was nothing else in the room.

Professor Chhaya, who wore a traditional *kurta* (long flowing shirt) and pajama, looked up at the sound of my footsteps. He grinned and motioned me to sit in the chair in front of his desk. A practicing architect, he was studiously working on a project report that echoed the vastu belief of maintaining harmony with nature. He was designing dwellings that would satisfy the requirements of villagers in Rajasthan, a neighboring state southwest of New Delhi.

"The Rajasthan government has built many houses for villagers, but they won't move in. Won't even enter them. Why?" Professor Chhaya was clearly irritated, but he didn't expect me to answer. "Simply because a house should evolve out of nature." The Rajasthan government fails to grasp this concept—a problem that is endemic with all Indian state governments.

Professor Chhaya was a typical Indian intellectual, with an expressive face and graceful hands that enunciated his words. He loved to speak, and his elegance and intelligence made you listen. In my case, I also had no choice. He immediately announced that he would not answer ANY question about vastu until I understood some important aspects of Vedic philosophy, which gave rise to the science. More to the point, he told me to be quiet until he thought I was ready to learn about vastu.

After a few hours, he had scraped away the top layer of my ignorance. I felt launched into intellectually fertile terrain. Professor Chhaya sent me off with reading lists that included books involving the *Vedas* (spiritual texts that form the backbone of Hinduism) and some of his carefully saved lecture notes. He also sent me off to meet Sudesh Prabhakar, an architect and frequent guest lecturer at New Delhi's School of Planning and Architecture.

Sudesh worked in Saket, a community in New Delhi that I knew extremely well. I had lived in Saket for eight years—just one block away from Sudesh, as it turns out. Sudesh's office was on the second floor of a government-constructed building that had put a stranglehold on aesthetics and promoted mold and mildew over maintenance and, most likely, vastu.

When I met Sudesh, he was casually dressed in khakis and an open-collared Western-style shirt. He waved me into his cramped office. He was in the midst of a phone conversation. When he put down the receiver, I blurted out the reason for my visit: "Professor Chhaya says that you are the best person to teach me about vastu."

Sudesh asked an office worker to bring us some tea. He said that he had been out of his office most of the day and his eyes lowered to go over the list of phone calls that had come in during his absence. By the time he looked up again, his reading glasses had slid to the bridge of his nose. Sudesh peered over their rim at me. His round face wore a sly expression that quickly softened into a smile.

I laughed before Sudesh did. I knew that my opening line was a thinly veiled question, the equivalent of my asking the President of the United States for access to the vaults at Fort Knox. Tea arrived.

Small talk about the neighborhood and then silence filled the room before Sudesh said that he was not impressed by most of the new books on vastu. They were inconsistent and too closely linked with superstition. Vastu, he believes, is a tool to help us achieve harmony with the universe and our particular environment. Vastu cannot prevent the troubles that occur in a life. Vastu can only cushion the fall.

Sudesh looked again at me as if to analyze where I fit inside this revival in vastu. He smiled, and his dark eyes were bright as onyx. His suspicion about people who took a sudden interest in vastu without even reading the ancient texts clearly extended to me, a foreigner, who now sat across from him. He said that he needed a week to think about my request, then called for another cup of tea.

Sudesh was easy to like. He had a generous laugh and a powerful enthusiasm that exploded out of his short frame. There was nothing false or pretentious about the man. His office was a mess, but it was obvious that he didn't care. He shuffled through papers on his desk and would marvel at the discovery of something he needed in the clutter. Sudesh also loved books. We were surrounded by part of his collection—mainly books on architecture and Indian philosophy. I longed to glance at pages that he had flagged with bright pink Post-Its, but his library was not yet open to me. Sudesh needed to get to know me.

By the end of our second cup of tea, forty-five-year-old Sudesh had rattled off some of the important facts of his life. How he was passionate about all schools of architecture. How he had lived as a youngster in England and had traveled widely. Just his mention of visits to Venice, Paris, and London changed the expression on his face and conveyed his thoughts. I could see him soaking in the architectural magnificence that added character to these cities. Sudesh was even more enamored by Indian architecture, and by the *Vedas*, in particular the *Upanisads*, the concluding wisdom and philosophy that ended each of these sacred Hindu books.

Indeed, it was Sudesh's spiritualism, which included nearly twenty years of practicing yoga and meditation, that brought him to vastu about fifteen years ago. Once he started reading the ancient texts on vastu, he came to appreciate the spiritual aspects of great Indian architecture. Through his own spiritual growth, Sudesh came in touch with his own personal philosophy. "If you don't see the beauty of the universe, you can never love it," he said, with iron conviction. And Sudesh, who insisted that he was an architect who wants to bring a spiritual aspect into architecture, was a man inspired by his love of the universe and all that it contained.

I had such a focused objective—getting Sudesh to help me on my quest to discover vastu—that during my first two meetings with him I never noticed the effect that his office had on me. I only noticed the activities that would interrupt our conversation. A phone rang and Sudesh answered it. Faxes would require his immediate attention. He proofread letters and sent them back for a final draft, examined and modified architectural drawings—normal procedures for any busy architect and his staff.

At our third meeting, Sudesh decided that he would help me learn about vastu. The tension that vibrated inside me vanished, and finally I noticed what I had failed to see earlier. Sudesh's employees, mainly architectural assistants and a young man who served as receptionist, overlord of the kitchen, and locator of lost files, were always in a good mood. The office revolved around a healthy interaction that included mutual respect, and everyone, including Sudesh, seemed consistently focused on work.

It was at this point that I also saw beyond the stacks of books, files, and tools of the trade that defined Sudesh's office. I realized that I was in a room that followed vastu guidelines. Wherever the room's construction was not in order, Sudesh had placed a tiny symbol to correct the defect. The symbol was a spiraling *swastika*, a Vedic symbol of well-being and auspiciousness that was cynically and successfully corrupted by Hitler. The Sanskrit word even means well-being. I knew that there was no way this maligned symbol could be reused in the West, where emotional associations are still so powerful; but in India, this old symbol maintained its original potency and was ingrained in the Hindu culture.

The approximately twelve-foot by twelve-foot room was modest, yet it was rich in tranquility. The room was too small to create an obvious empty center space, which is important in vastu, but it was there—a tiny bit of emptiness between my feet and the legs of Sudesh's desk. The heaviest load in the office, a built-in cupboard stuffed with more books and files, was properly placed in the room's southwest. And Sudesh faced east, the direction of enlightenment, when he worked at his desk—the same direction that I faced when I slowly waded through my stack of Vedic books.

On top of Sudesh's computer, which was about a foot away from his desk, sat a small carving of the Laughing Buddha with his arms thrust joyfully into the air. Buddha appeared to be keeping an eye on Sudesh and his visitors. This particular Buddha was an apt symbol for a man who clearly enjoyed life.

Sudesh asked me hard questions that subtly reinforced his belief, one shared by Professor Chhaya, that to understand vastu, I had to understand its link to other Hindu disciplines. I also had to understand the core philosophy that supports each discipline—the philosophy of the *Vedas* and especially, the *Upanisads*. By the time Sudesh decided that he trusted me, a strange foreigner with an unlikely mission, I also knew that he was the appropriate person to teach me about vastu. It was such a quirk of fate—not unusual in India. A neighbor, one that I had never met when we lived up the road from one another, had agreed to help me on the quest that not only brought me back to India, but a block away from my old home in Saket.

PART ONE

THE JOURNEY

When a man does not realize his kinship with the world,
he lives in a prison whose walls are alien to him.
When he meets the eternal spirit in all objects,
then is he emancipated, for then he discovers the fullest
significance of the world into which he is born; then
he finds himself in perfect truth, and his harmony
with the all is established.

—RABINDRANATH TAGORE, *SADHANA*

❧ 1 ❧

THE VEDAS AND VASTU

I am the sapidity in water; I am the light in the moon
and the sun; I am the syllable OM in all the Vedas,
sound in ether, and virility in men; I am the sweet
fragrance in earth and the brilliance in fire, the life in all
beings, and I am austerity in the austere. Know me as
the eternal seed of all beings; I am the intelligence of the
intelligent; the splendor of the splendid am I.

BHAGAVAD GITA, VII: 8,9,10

T HE WORD *VASTU*, which derives from Hinduism's sacred texts, the
Vedas, means "a dwelling or site." Originally, vastu was used in city
planning, temples for the gods, and palaces, forts, and residences for
the Hindu upper classes. But today's vastu applies to any dwelling, from a
palatial home to a modest studio apartment, a huge loft, a cabin on a lake,
or a factory or office building.

The theories that support vastu and all the other Hindu disciplines, such
as yoga and ayurveda, arise from the four-volume *Vedas* (the Sanskrit word
veda means "knowledge," from the word *ved*, "to know"). Hinduism was originally called *Sanatana Dharma*, which means "eternal faith." Daily practice of

one's *dharma* (duty) keeps one on the path that leads to the liberation of the soul from the recurring cycles of life and death. Through the practice of all these Hindu (Vedic) disciplines, an individual can move toward the awakening of the true self and the realization that the internal essence or soul is part of the Supreme Creative Force.

Within this vast body of Vedic wisdom, four essential theories put forth in the *Upanisads,* the concluding wisdom that ends each of the sacred *Vedas,* are pivotal to the understanding of Hinduism and these disciplines:

1. the law of nature creates an undeniable order and harmony in the universe;
2. everything that exists (meaning all universal phenomena) is animated;
3. all existence is interconnected;
4. the essence of everything is part of That—the Supreme Creative Force.

This last point touches on one of the central truths explained in the great Vedic texts: *Tat Tvam Asi,* or Thou Art That; "That" being a part of the indefinable, unfathomable Supreme Creative Force, however you choose to define it. The Supreme Creative Force lies not just beyond the body and beyond the scope of our limited vision: The Supreme Creative Force lies within us. The individual essence held within the body—and the body is merely matter that is born and decays—is part of the unseen Supreme Creative Force.

This powerful theory that arrives at Tat Tvam Asi is echoed in all the Hindu disciplines from vastu and yoga to classical Indian music and ayurveda. Aldous Huxley in his introduction to the important Hindu epic, *Bhagavad-Gita,* describes this Vedic theory as "one of the clearest and most comprehensive summaries of the Perennial Philosophy ever to have been made. Hence its enduring value, not only for Indians, but for all mankind."[3]

[3] Swami Prabhavananda and Christopher Isherwood, trans. *The Song of God: Bhagavad-Gita,* Aldous Huxley, intro. (New York: New American Library, July 1993).

FOUR ESSENTIAL VEDIC THEORIES

1. THE LAW OF NATURE

The Vedic law of nature sees an innate order and harmony in the universe. Nothing man-made should interfere with this governing principle. This is where vastu comes in. There is nothing random in creation and nothing random about the design of any created form. Everything that exists in the natural world is endowed with an appropriate proportion and rhythm that gives grace and beauty to all creation.

Each created object or form has its function, its place in the mysterious scheme of the cosmos. If the harmony or order of the cosmos is disturbed, the result is chaos, disharmony, and an absence of well-being for all existence, from the mountains and rivers to every single creature, right down to the tiniest organism.

This principle of absolute harmony and order in the universe is the governing rule behind the science of vastu. Violate the law of nature in the design of your home and you end up without harmony—and frequently with an architectural eyesore! Violate the law of nature *within* your home or workspace and you will feel the same absence of harmony. Pay heed to the law of nature and you will find harmony and inner peace. You will have created a loving home for the soul.

2. EVERYTHING THAT EXISTS IS ANIMATED

The Vedic texts say that everything in the universe is living. Everything vibrates and pulsates. Quantum physics accepts this now as well. Within Vedic philosophy, two terms define the process that gives a specific form to invisible energy: *prakriti* and *purusha*.

Prakriti and Purusha

Prakriti is what we can see. It is the principle that creates all matter and determines its constitution or nature. For example, prakriti determines our specific physical, mental and emotional constitution, which then shapes our nature and behavior. Prakriti, an active force, unites with purusha, which is passive. Purusha represents the animating principle within all matter. It is the spirit, the soul, the energy that causes matter to pulsate or vibrate. And all matter does vibrate.

In other words, prakriti provides the material aspects of our body, while purusha represents the unseen spirit or energy. The ultimate goal is to liberate the purusha from the confines of prakriti. After all, our body—prakriti—is bound by time. But purusha is formless and eternal. In one of the *Upanisads*, the soul is referred to as *neti*, or that which cannot be described.[4]

It is our human form, our body or prakriti, that we can see and describe, not our soul. The soul is the energy/essence/purusha contained within matter/body/prakriti. Today, evidence from biology and physics supports this Vedic theory of animation (or pulsation) and the relationship between energy and matter. Through research, geobiologists and physicists know that a flower, a wall, a single cell viewed under the microscope—every single form—vibrates and emits its own wavelength.

While Vedic sages did not use the contemporary terminology of wavelengths and vibrations, ancient vastu guidelines make it clear that these spiritual scientists understood the principles attached to invisible energies, which they defined as cosmic energy. These spiritual scientists, including vastu architects, also understood that every life form responds to and interacts with these vibrations, which can have either a negative or positive influence on any pulsating form, including the human body.

We are normally unaware of vibrations unless they have a reasonable audible magnitude, such as a loud wail or a piercing whistle, or unless we see them—a ripple on a pond or the quivering of a piano string. But vibrations

---

[4] Max Muller, trans. and commentaries "Brahadaaranyaka Upanisad" in the *Upanisads*, Vol. 2 (New York: Dover Publications, 1989).

surround us. Put your hand against the speaker of your stereo as it plays music. Your hand will feel the vibrations of the sound.

These observations play a critical role in vastu. Since energy causes everything to vibrate, then it naturally follows that vibrations exist on our property, in our home, and in our workspace—in all architecture—as well as within us. Any space that conforms to vastu guidelines aims to maintain or even enhance the flow of positive vibrations and attempts to block out negative vibrations. The objective is to make the building's vibrations resonate or harmonize with the surrounding environment and with the vibrations of the inhabitants of the structure.

Everything should be in consonance and working together. Nothing should be in opposition. This is what increases our spiritual well-being, protects our physical and mental health, and, some say, brings about wealth.

The Power of Vibrations

To demonstrate that interactions with vibrations can be negative or positive, consider experiments that show that plants respond affirmatively to the sound of classical music. The plants' positive interactions with the vibrations created by the music increased their growth. Or consider how an extremely high-pitched human voice can shatter a crystal glass or hurt our ears. Vibrations clearly have the power to create, preserve, or destroy. Understanding this principle is critical to vastu. When we design a space, our goal should be to enhance positive vibrations and shut out negative vibrations. When external vibrations interact with our own, our goal is to have the interactions be harmonized and therefore beneficial to us.

3. WE ARE ALL INTERCONNECTED

Vedic texts assert that everything in the universe is interconnected—from an unnamed star to a newborn baby. Nothing exists in isolation. On one level this is a holistic theory; but in the Vedic texts and vastu, this concept assumes a spiritual dimension. Vastu and the Vedic philosophy connect this sense of wholeness to the principle that we must respect and preserve all creation. As with the links in a mesh chain, let one link break and the chain breaks. When the chain breaks, we all suffer as a result.

Historically, the practice of vastu showed a profound and unlimited respect for all matter. If timber was required in the construction of a building, each chosen tree was sanctified. Creatures inhabiting a tree were entreated to leave so that no harm would come to them. The ax was washed before it was used. A text on vastu even describes an ancient rule that each fallen tree should be sheltered for six months so that it could heal from its wounds. Only then could the tree be used for construction. Stones themselves and any life form that were disturbed in the removal of stones received the same respect, reverence, and careful handling.[5]

The Vedic philosophy and vastu hold that every form within the universe is nothing less than a manifestation of the different aspects of the Supreme Creator. Our respect and reverence for everything that exists is reinforced by our acknowledgment that the essence of all matter is connected to the Supreme Creative Force.

It follows, then, that not only should we respect our environment and revere the beauty in its creation, but we should also respect ourselves and treat the outer body and the inner self with care and kindness. Our soul, or atma, is no exception. It is important to understand that the goal of seeking inner peace, even while we are going through our cycle of existence, is to recognize the true self so that it can merge with That.

4. THE ESSENCE OF EVERYTHING IS PART OF THAT

And how does this fourth belief—that the essence of everything is part of That—relate to vastu? Vastu's primary objective in the creation of buildings intended for our personal use (as opposed to the creation of temples that

---

[5] Dr. Balagopal T. S. Prahbu and Dr. A. Achyuthan, *Vatavidyapravesi: A Textbook of Vastuvidya* (Calicut: Vastuvidyapratisthanam, 1996).

honor the gods) is the design of perfect spaces that will nurture the human soul, which, again, is a part of the Essence of the Supreme Creative Force.

THE VEDIC CULTURE: WHEN DID IT BEGIN?

There is great debate about the dates of the culture that worshipped the *Vedas* and practiced the Vedic philosophy and way of life. Until recently it was believed that the Vedic culture developed around 2500 BC. But in recent decades, scholars have been examining previously overlooked or discounted geographic and time-related references in the collection of hymns called the *Rig-Veda*, the most important of the four sacred *Vedas*, as well as reassessing findings from archaeological sites. Some scholars now put the date much earlier—as early as 6000 BC.[6]

Besides the conflict over the dates, Hindus also believe that the *Vedas* have no authorship and no beginning or end. One great book on the *Vedas* explains that the *Vedas* are the coexisting breath of the Paramaatma, the unmanifested soul of the Supreme Creative Force or Brahman. The manifested Supreme Creative Force, which has no beginning or end, remains in a state of perpetual existence. The perpetual existence also extends to the *Vedas*, the life-sustaining breath of the Supreme Creative Force. Neither one created the other. They co-exist and their co-existence is eternal.[7]

Many Hindu myths speak of the "arrival" of the *Vedas*. But myths, as we know, are parables created as assessable interpretations of metaphysical beliefs. They are stories in which any reference can be historic fact or fiction. One popular myth states that the *Vedas* actually guided the manifested form of Brahman or the Supreme Creator, the Hindu Lord Brahma, in his creation of the universe. After Lord Brahma finished his task, he rested a few

---

[6] See David Frawley, *Gods, Sages and Kings: Vedic Secrets of Ancient Civilization* (Salt Lake City: Passage Press, 1991).
[7] Sri Chandrasekharendra Sawaswati, *The Vedas* (Mumbai: Bharatiya Vidya Bhavan, Sudakshina Trust, 1998).

undefined eons until he then passed on the Vedic knowledge to certain select *rishis* (seers), who lived in the world of mortals.

These chosen rishis were the only mortals who had attained enough spiritual enlightenment so that they could hear Lord Brahma's pure vibrations. These vibrations converted into sound, which the rishis, in turn, converted into the words of the *Vedas*. The underlying theory is that rishis, through their rigorous self-discipline, acquired such power over their own breath and became so spiritually enlightened that they could hear the cosmic breath or the vibrations of the *Vedas*. The Supreme Creative Force or Brahman, which coexists with the *Vedas* and shares the state of perpetual existence, then created Lord Brahma so that He, as the Lord of Creation, could create the universe. Neither the universe nor Lord Brahma, however, is beyond the cycle of life and death. Neither one exists beyond the world controlled by time.

THE CREATIVE FORCE OF AUM

Hinduism isn't the only religion with such a conception of the power of sound. The Christian Bible's New Testament Gospel of St. John opens: "In the beginning was the Word, and the Word was with God, and the Word was God." In Hinduism, however, the primordial word is AUM or OM, meaning "first created." Pure energy, which leads to the vibrations that create the primordial and ever-existing word AUM, becomes the impetus behind all that is created and continues to be created.

The concept of AUM ties directly into vastu. The objective of vastu is to build man-made creations that mirror the perfection of the universe, and since the universe started with the primordial word AUM, vastu also pays attention to the effects of the sounds or vibrations that exist on a site and in a building, and even within the building's occupants. Vastu works to keep all these vibrations in harmony.

CREATION, PRESERVATION AND DISSOLUTION

According to Vedic philosophy the universe moves through an endless cycle of creation, preservation, and dissolution. AUM is the creative phase of the cycle. Those new to yoga and meditation may be familiar with this word, but not its relevance. According to Swami Chinmayananda, one of the great Hindu philosophers who left behind comprehensive commentaries on the *Vedas* and the *Upanisads*, it is the silence (or breath) that follows the concluding *M* in AUM that gives this word its potency. Any chant or mantra that does not include AUM with its concluding breath, lacks power. Indeed, the completion of the word AUM with the obligatory breath is no less important than the breath that gives life to all existence. We all know that the cessation of breath means the end of life.[8]

Swami Chinmayananda expresses more layers to AUM's vast symbolism. The word's three letters represent the entire range of the creation of articulated sound. Utterances either originate in the throat, somewhere within the cavity of the mouth, or on the tip of one's lips. With the correct pronunciation of AUM, the throat makes the sound of *A*—the beginning point of sound creation. As with the letter *A*, the formation of *U* starts at the throat, but then rolls right through the mouth to the tip of the lips. Pressing together the lips creates the sound of *M* in AUM. This final letter represents the limit to articulated sound and leads ultimately to silence, which is equally potent. With the proper articulation of AUM, the word symbolizes the Hindu concept of the creation (*A*), preservation (*U*), and dissolution (*M*) of the universe.

AUM is nothing less than the essence of the Supreme Creator who first uttered the Word that is the force behind the three actions of creation, preservation, and dissolution. AUM is so sacred that the symbol of the word is rarely placed on the floor, and it is never stepped on. Properly recited during meditation, AUM produces within the one who meditates a sense of inner peace. If one is truly committed to the practice of meditation

---

[8] Swami Chinmayananda, *Art of God Symbolism* (Mumbai: Central Chinmaya Mission Trust, 1987).

25

or yoga, the Word can open up a transmission between the self and the Supreme Creator.

FIGURE 1

Symbol of AUM

A scientist may dismiss these assertions as nothing more than blind belief in spiritual theory, but science has already proven the power of sound, as mentioned previously in the discussion of the experiments that have been performed on plants. Other studies have shown that babies in the womb benefit from the vibrations they receive from classical music.

The rishis, who heard the holy vibrations of the *Vedas* during some unknown period of time, chose to pass on their information orally from generation to generation. Finally, Veda Vyasa, a poet and philosopher who many scholars believe wrote the *Mahabharata* (one of the great Hindu epics) and possibly wrote or codified eighteen of the popular volumes of mythology called the *Puranas* (ancient stories), organized the *Vedas* into the four volumes that exist today.

Many of these same scholars suggest that this great rishi arranged the verses sometime between 2500 BC and 1500 BC. (Most dates that are connected to Hindu philosophy and attributed to a time before the advent of Christianity are mired in dispute.) In the process, Vyasa also created the inspiring meter and rhythm that exist throughout the sacred books in the same way that rhythm flows through every Vedic discipline from vastu to music. Vyasa's work preserved the *Vedas* (at least that portion of the *Vedas* heard by the rishis) for generations to come.

VEDIC PHILOSOPHY AND SCIENCE

It bears repeating that the *Vedas*, especially the *Upanisads*, are a total amalgamation of spirituality and science. And many of the scientific discoveries expressed in the Vedic texts present a marvel of accuracy. Vedic mathematicians developed the revolutionary concept of the zero; and this early civilization not only was aware of the impact of vibrations on all matter but also had a sophisticated understanding of the inner workings of the universe.

Thousands of years before Newton, Vedic scholars had theories about the law of gravity and other notions about physics that predate the West's. They understood how gravitational forces knit the solar system together and had a serious effect on our planet. They understood long before anyone else that the earth was not flat but spherical in shape. They figured out that the earth revolved around the sun long before the Greek mathematician Pythagoras, who lived about 497 BC, and the sixteenth-century astronomer Nicholaus Copernicus.

Vedic scholars also had an astonishing grasp of the probable evolution of the universe that is close to present-day speculation. They intuited cycles of creation and destruction in the universe, and speculated that these cycles took place over eons of time. The world, they theorized, took ages to be built, far longer than the Judeo-Christian notion of seven days. The universe, they speculated, exists for trillions of years—a period of time that represents the life span of Lord Brahma, who is the manifested form of Brahman and the creator of the universe. When His life cycle is completed, the life cycle of the universe also comes to an end. It is destroyed to be reborn with the rebirth of Lord Brahma, who begins the slow process of evolution once again.

ORIGINS OF VASTU

Vastu is mentioned within Vedic texts, but its actual evolution is as difficult to trace as the origins of the *Vedas*. Looking at mythology, one story about vastu insists that, along with the *Vedas*, vastu existed before Lord Brahma created the universe. Lord Brahma needed the finest architect to design a perfect master plan. Nothing could ever rival the creation of the universe, although all subsequent architecture should attempt to match the beauty, utility, and durability of this divine creation.

A popular legend claims that Lord Brahma gave the knowledge of vastu to the Hindu god Shiva, who then passed it on to Vishwakarma, who was known as the celestial architect. The mention of Vishwakarma begins to overlap with history. Some authors of sixth-century AD vastu *sastras*, or treatises, claim that their texts are based on the laws devised by an ancient sage named Vishwakarma. Vishwakarma is also mentioned in many of the Hindu collections of mythology, called *Puranas*, and his name and the names of his creations appear in the great Hindu epics, the *Ramayana* and the *Mahabharata*.

Possibly the first written discussion of vastu appears in the *Stapatya Veda*, a part of the *Atharva Veda*, which was the fourth and final *Veda* to be codified. Actual vastu sastras, which were compiled as early as the sixth century AD, and provide guidelines for the design and construction of towns, palaces, forts, simple dwellings, temples, furniture, and icons, have been discovered in various regions of present-day India. The two most important compilations found to date were written in the tenth century AD, the *Manasara Series*, which was written by Rishi Manasara, and the eleventh century *Mayamata*, which was written by the brilliant *acharya* (highly respected teacher) and architect Maya. This period also overlaps with the golden age of temple and palace construction in India, and many of these extraordinary buildings were clearly designed as per vastu.

The *Manasara Series* and the *Mayamata* provide us with a detailed account of the guidelines that govern the proper selection of a site on which to create a

28

building. They describe soil test experiments to determine the suitability of the land for construction. To determine the quality of the soil, the builder was instructed to create a cavity in the site, which he then refilled with the same soil. If the soil did not refill the cavity, the site should be rejected. It could not support the strength of a construction. If the soil refilled the cavity, the quality of the soil was fair, not particularly special. But if the soil was so plentiful that it spilled over the cavity, the site was ideal. This soil was firm and compact; it would not settle or shift under the weight of a building after construction.

To determine if there was adequate underground water for a well, the builder was to dig an area in the site to the depth of a man standing with his arms held straight above his head. If the site hit water at that depth, this indicated adequate water. To determine if a site was too arid, the builder was advised to dig out some of the site and fill it with water. If there was no water left, the soil was too dry. If most of the water remained, the site was too moist and should be rejected. If some of the water remained in the hole twenty-four hours later, the soil was potentially good.

These tests to analyze the soil quality and water availability were highly logical. And throughout the texts, scientific reasoning flowed right along with spiritual beliefs. Placement and orientation of a dwelling for a mortal or deity, commentaries about construction of furniture and conveyances that were used back then—all reveal common sense and reinforce Vedic theories about creation.

After all, creation of a man-made structure for the gods or kings or the simplest mortal had to strive for the perfection exhibited in the creation of the universe. Architects and their craftsmen had to follow the example of the celestial architect, Vishwakarma, and adhere to the principles of order and harmony and all the other pillars of the Vedic philosophy.

RITUALS

All this also helps to explain why the ancient practice of vastu—from the choice of the site to the completion of the building—involved the observance of numerous rituals. There were rituals to entreat former spirits to leave a site before it was disturbed and there were numerous rituals to bless the gods. All these rituals, with their *mantras*, or incantations, set in motion the proper vibrations that were necessary in all creation.

Blessings to the gods were usually complex offerings of various matter found on earth, from different kinds of soil to the most precious of precious jewels. These offerings were a form of acknowledgment of the spiritual and scientific laws of the universe that prevailed over a man-made vastu creation. By making an offering and through careful adherence to the guidelines, the architect was showing his respect for the forces and elements that exist in this perfect universe created by Lord Brahma, which was the model for the architect's own creation.

ENHANCING SPIRITUAL GROWTH

Vastu never loses sight of Vedic philosophy, never forgets that man-made environments must be created that ultimately help, not hinder, an individual living the principles of Hinduism: *Sanatana Dharma*, the Eternal Faith. The built space must have an environment that allows the occupants to carry out their dharma and move toward the difficult attainment of enlightenment and the liberation of the soul. This explains why the vastu sastras even offered guidelines for the creation of religious icons. Every icon was to be perfect, without any defect, and to reach this level of perfection, vastu architects devised their own measuring system that used the *tala* (the size of a typical human palm or face) as the appropriate measurement to create the perfect rhythm and proportion of the manifestation of the deity.

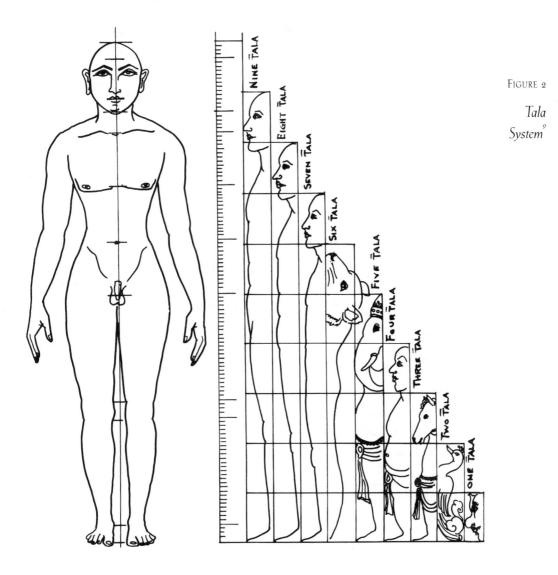

FIGURE 2

Tala System[9]

The sastras also described acceptable themes for paintings so that the mind dwells on positive thoughts that lead toward the divine:

[9] This drawing is based on the drawing in the following book: Prasanna Kumar Acharya, ed. and trans. *Architecture of Manasara, Illustrations of Architectural and Sculptural Objects, Manasara Series: Vol. V* (New Delhi: Munshiram Manoharlal Publishers Pvt. Ltd., 1994).

Representations of joyous scenes and religious images are proper. . . . Battle scenes and images of death and misfortune should not appear there nor representations of combat between gods and demons, neither pictures of naked mendicants, of the love play of ascetics nor of suffering people.[10]

VASTU AND ARTISTIC FREEDOM

This huge compendium of guidelines, however, never restricted the talent of an architect. Vastu sastras served to insure the proper proportion and rhythm of all buildings and built forms. Any analysis of India's ancient temples and palaces that were designed according to vastu reveals remarkable architectural freedom and artistry. Unlike Western treatises on architecture, the original Sanskrit books of vastu sastras didn't have any architectural drawings that would suggest that an architect had to follow a specific design as per an accompanying illustration. My teacher Sudesh points out that drawings were added to the English translations.

Sudesh also insists that the great vastu texts, such as the *Manasara* or the *Mayamata*, assumed that change would occur in architecture along with an individual's growth in personal awareness and society's advancement in technology. "An architect was supposed to be creative," insists Sudesh. "That's why no two Indian temples are exactly alike. The sastras are not a noose around your neck. They're words that help you fly."

THE FIVE ELEMENTS

To understand vastu, we must understand the Vedic theory of the composition of the universe. To create the universe, the Spiritual Creative Force (Brahman) assumed the manifested form of Lord Brahma, the Creator, who

[10] Kapila Vatsyayan, general ed. and Bruno Dagens, trans., *Mayamata, Vol. I* (Delhi: Indira Gandhi National Centre for the Arts in association with Motilal Banarsidass Publishers, 1994).

created the five basic elements out of his own essence. First came space; from space came air; from air came fire; from fire came water; and from water came earth.

With the evolution of each element, each successive element contained the property of each of the preceding elements. Space only contained space, but air contained air and space. This absorption continued through the fifth element of earth, which also contained space, air, fire, and water. And all five of these elements are involved in the creation of all matter.

Scientists accept that all phenomena contain a combination or compounds of these five elements. But since these elements are not irreducible, they have created a modern periodic table of elements, which is still not considered definitive, and includes the quarks and the electrons in a list that presently exceeds one hundred.

According to vastu, the five basic elements of space, air, fire, water, and earth are everywhere—inside us and around us—and the presence of each element is beneficial to us. Looking specifically at the elements within us, digestive fire helps break down the food that we eat and burns the calories that give us energy. The flow of air inhaled during the act of breathing pumps the blood through our system and keeps us alive. Nearly two thirds of our body is made of a composition that includes water. Without the presence of water, none of us could survive.

From conception, our body requires space and continues to need space throughout its existence. And the quality of earth is present in our bones and in all our vital minerals, such as zinc and iron, that keep us healthy. According to vastu, these same five elements are also present in the forms that we call architecture. Each of the elements has a representative deity, and together, they share a predetermined location on the site, in the building, and again in each room. Brahma represents the element of space; Vayu, the element of air; Agni, the element of fire; Isa, the element of water; and Pitri, the element of earth.

Honoring the elements, with their deities, honors the laws of nature. Honoring the elements also honors the order and harmony that governs the perfect universe. Vastu prevents a problem or corrects a problem by making certain that each element and its deity are not disturbed. To disregard this vastu principle spells trouble. Sudesh would frequently say: "Ignore a deity's proper space is to ask for a civil war." A civil war among deities is no small thing and the helpless occupants of the built space are the unfortunate victims.

CONTROLLING POSITIVE AND NEGATIVE FORCES

In recent years, geobiologists have been studying the impact of electric and magnetic fields that they claim can interfere with our health and deplete our energy. While the ancient vastu texts do not mention these fields by name, many geobiologists believe that vastu sages understood the potential harm connected to these fields. The basic elements, allocated their appropriate space in a site and in construction, serve as a counter-force that offers us protection from these negative sources.

In the process of enclosing an open space, construction can also disrupt access to sunrays and the free flow of positive energies, or trap negative energies inside the building. Even alterations or remodeling in a preexisting structure, from adding a room to introducing a new color scheme or shifting around the furniture, can have profound repercussions that effect the flow of energies and their relationship to the interior space and our own energies.

Vastu takes all of these factors into consideration and creates a space where there is a beneficial interaction between the vibrations of the occupants and the positive vibrations that are allowed to flow with minimum interference throughout the site and its dwelling. This healthy flow of positive vibrations complements the vibrations that exist within the pulsating human form. Conversely, vastu guidelines appease, block, or even remove the harmful vibrations that dilute our positive vibrations and wear us down.

THE POWER OF THE SUN

Vastu also understands that solar dynamics affect our well-being. Accordingly, vastu guidelines maximize the sun's positive effects and decrease the sun's negative effects. In Hindu mythology, Surya, the sun god, rides a chariot pulled by seven horses or deities as he makes his daily journey across the horizon from east to west. The deities are said to be the seven rays of the sun. While these deities are part of Hindu mythology, scientifically they represent the seven visible colors of the spectrum: violet, indigo, blue, green, yellow, orange, and red.

Vastu believes that the rays of the sun should filter into a building during the morning when sunlight is neither too bright nor too hot. Indeed, yogis believe that the best rays of the sun come just before we recognize the dawn. This is the ideal time to practice yoga and receive maximum rejuvenation. But in general, morning rays are positive; afternoon rays are negative. Think about the intense heat that accompanies the sun between one and five on a summer's afternoon and how it feels when it pours into a room. Doesn't it make you feel uncomfortable? Doesn't it sap you of your energy?

VASTU: THE FIRST ENVIRONMENTAL SCIENCE

All these vastu theories involving the elements, solar dynamics, vibrations, and universal forces were applied from the time of the Vedic Age to the foundation of design and architecture for structures, and also determined city planning. Vastu's primary concern with the interrelationship of organisms and their environments conceivably makes vastu the oldest holistic architectural discipline and the precursor to the contemporary science of ecology.

Vastu's guidelines were consistently environmentally sound. The practitioner would always remember that while the external elements and energies are inherently constant, the elements and energies within an interior space are not. The practitioner knew that any alteration in the relationship between the existing energies and the interior space could influence the harmony of the elements. This influence effects the occupants of the space.

REDISCOVERING THE SOUL

How we treat all these forces when we set up a home or a workspace has significant consequences—good or bad—on our soul, that single part of us that is everlasting and eternal. Vastu understands this. It also understands that through the course of our earthly existence, our soul also becomes so buried and so far removed from its original connection to the Supreme Creator that we must work hard to rid ourselves of all the sheathes or layers of earthly interference. Unless our home is conducive to inward thinking that leads us to this crucial realization, we can never really find an everlasting inner peace. But vastu spaces are designed so that we can begin this process. These spaces exist as the healthy bridge between the outer world and the inner world. In the next two chapters, we will see just how vastu fulfills this objective, in a home designed for mortals and in a "home" designed for the gods.

✳ 2 ✳

THE VASTU PURUSHA MANDALA

Nothing can work without rules. The entire solar system would go
to pieces if there were even a momentary breach of the rules governing it.

—MAHATMA GANDHI

EASTERN RELIGIONS—Hinduism, Jainism, Buddhism, Taoism—all use
mandalas as visual aids for meditation. Constructed on a complex grid
of interlinking squares and circles, these spiritual diagrams represent
an elaborately symbolic view of the universe. While the whole mandala is
often in the shape of a circle, the celestial realm of the gods rests within an
interior square, which is frequently called a palace or a temple. A manifestation of a deity, either wrathful—so that it can overcome evil and help a
devotee focus on the right thoughts that guide one along the path to
enlightenment—or benign, is normally prominent within the square. Some

mandalas focus on a powerful symbol, such as the lotus flower, as the central point of concentration.

On a deeper level, a mandala serves as a tool and guide to enlightenment. A good number of mandalas have four gateways, one in each of the four cardinal directions. These gates lead to the pure realm within. The individual meditates on the outer circles to prepare for the transformation that allows him insight into the layers of wisdom held inside the square temple. As part of the process, the individual chants a particular mantra connected to the mandala, which is usually associated with the deity who is portrayed within the sacred realm. Repeated chanting of the mantra evokes the divine presence of the deity, and it is at this moment that one gains access to the deepest wisdom that is guarded and protected inside the pure realm.

FIGURE 3

*Vastu Purusha
Mandala*

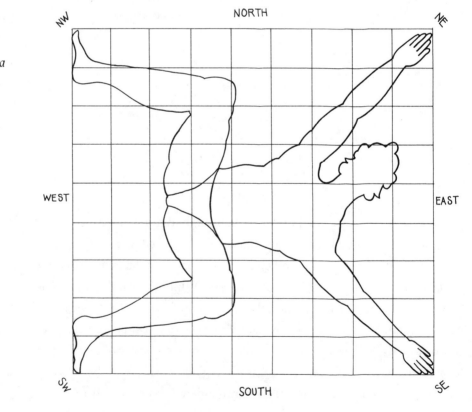

The vastu purusha mandala was not created as an object of meditation; it is, however, a representation of the Hindu view of the universe, and it holds much of the wisdom contained in the practice of vastu. By paying careful attention to this diagram, we can create a nurturing home and nurturing place to work. On the other hand, it is said that if we ignore the important principles conveyed through the diagram, we compromise our well-being and show disrespect for all creation. In sum, the vastu purusha mandala is a Vedic architectural blueprint—the key to vastu success.

To understand the vastu purusha mandala, we need to remember that the Sanskrit word *vastu* means "land or site." The Sanskrit word *purusha* means "the unseen spirit or energy." When these two words are brought together, they create a new concept: *vastu purusha*, where purusha extends life to vastu. The phrase means the cosmic spirit of the land or site.

VASTU PURUSHA

As always in Hinduism, the many myths connected to this spirit serve as important metaphors for the spiritual and scientific theories behind the practice of vastu. Here is one story about the cosmic spirit called vastu purusha.

Once there existed a thing that lacked form and name. This nameless and formless thing suddenly blocked both the sky and the earth in every direction, creating a dismal shield. The shield so alarmed the gods that they grabbed hold of this formless thing and forced it down to the earth.

Lord Brahma turned the formless thing into a spirit whose face was pressed into the ground. Brahma sat on the spirit's center, right over its navel, which is considered the center of the body, and, in Hinduism, is acknowledged as the source of all creation—providing the life-sustaining link between a mother and her child. Brahma instructed the other deities to sit on the rest of the creature so that it could never escape.

Brahma gave the form a name, vastu purusha, and said that if vastu purusha was not appeased before the start of construction on any plot of land, nothing but misfortune would be the fruit of such labor. Only when vastu purusha was appeased would the spirit bless and protect the construction. All would go well.

Appeasement of vastu purusha also means the appeasement of all the gods who are holding down the spirit. Each deity represents a function or a necessary piece in the grand machine that keeps the universe in working order. Therefore, the message of appeasement in this myth reminds us to obey the Vedic law of nature by following the vastu guidelines. The design and construction of a site must maintain harmony and order, revere and respect all phenomena. We must always remember that everything is interconnected, animate, and that the essence of all creation is a part of the essence of the Supreme Creator, who is the source of creation—in other words, Tat Tvam Asi or Thou Art That. The vastu purusha mandala is the blueprint that ensures environmentally sound and spiritually harmonious constructions and interior designs. Vastu turns every building into a holy space befitting its occupants.

THE SACRED SQUARE

The vastu purusha mandala can take the shape of various polygons; but the square is considered the most perfect form. The square symbolizes the Vedic view of the cosmos or universe. Its fixed and symmetrical form is an expression of the absolute harmony and balance that is present in the celestial realm. In *Hindu Temple*, one of the most respected books on Hindu temple architecture, Stella Kramrisch writes:

In the Hindu temple, it is the square Vedi [altar] which makes the sacred ground. The circular aspect of the earth is left behind, it belongs to the world of appearance and its movement; the earth is beheld itself under the perfection of the heavenly world and, knowing this perfection, is drawn as a square.[11]

The square shape of the Vedic altar used in Hindu rituals serves to sanctify the grounds on which the altar is constructed and to sanctify the altar itself. The Vedic altar is also constructed from earth, which is baked into bricks. In the baking process, the earth and its transformation into bricks are purified by fire. Therefore, the bricks that make the altar reinforce all the symbolism of the sacrificial fire that is ultimately ignited on the Vedic altar. The altar was the first step in the evolution of the temple. And every temple built according to the vastu guidelines also uses the square vastu purusha mandala to create a dwelling worthy of the gods.

FIGURE 4

Vedic Altar

THE HUMAN FORM

Vedic sages appreciated the orderly balance that exists in the ideal human form. They recognized that the measurement of the arms of a human extended to the right and left of the body equal the measurement of a human from the soles of the feet to the top of the head. Therefore, the

[11] Stella Kramrisch, *Hindu Temple, Vol. 1* (New Delhi: Motilal Banarsidass, 1995).

height and breadth of the human being also fits into a perfect square, the body mirroring the qualities of the universe. One of the most famous drawings by Leonardo Da Vinci, *Vetruvian Man*, illustrates these same theories.

FIGURE 5

Vedic Illustration of the Human Form

FIGURE 6

Da Vinci's Vitruvian Man

VASTU PURUSHA AND THE MANDALA

On the vastu purusha mandala, the image of the vastu purusha assumes the likeness of a man who is in a comfortable squatted position with his arms and legs reflecting a state of animation. Many new books on vastu show the deity with his face in the northeast. But the ancient texts of *Manasara* and *Mayamata* clearly indicate that the spirit's face is in the east. This direction is filled with good omens: enlightenment and truth, and the east receives the power of the sun.

Mayamata says:

> It should be known that the Spirit of the building has six bones (or lines), a single heart, four vulnerable points and four vessels (or diagonals) and that he lies upon the ground, his head in the east.[12]

Manasara further explains that the diagram shows the captured vastu purusha, face down, with his head in the east and tilted to the northeast, out of respect for Isa, the powerful deity who oversees the northeast quadrant— the gateway to the gods.[13] Lord Brahma is said to have faced this same sacred direction when he created the universe. And a man-made structure should strive for the perfection exhibited in Brahma's grand creation. To keep the spirit working in our best interests, *Vastu Living* uses the vastu purusha mandala with the spirit's head in the east.

[12] Kapila Vatsyayan, general ed. and Bruno Dagens, trans., *Mayamata Vol. 1* (Delhi: Indira Gandhi National Centre for the Arts in association with Motilal Banarsidass Publishers, 1994).
[13] Prasanna Kumar Acharya, ed. and trans. *Architecture of Manasara, Manasara Series: Vol. IV* (New Delhi: Munshiram Manoharlal Publishers Pvt. Ltd., 1994).

THE VULNERABLE POINTS OF VASTU PURUSHA

The English translation of the *Architecture of Manasara* describes the spirit, vastu purusha, as "hump-backed, crooked and lean."[14] Vastu practitioners believe that the *marmas*, or vulnerabilities, in the anatomy of vastu purusha mirror the vulnerable points in the human body. As such, specific joints and body parts of the spirit, such as the navel, heart, and lungs, must not be hurt during construction and must be considered in the interior design and location of the furniture in a room. Most of these points are in the center of the vastu purusha mandala, which is called the *Brahmasthana*.

Diagonal lines on the vastu purusha mandala are parallel to the nerves and the arteries, which are the channels of energy that run through the spirit's body and through our house. Because of their function, these lines of energy should be carefully considered in the construction of a space. The vastu purusha needs energy to flow through its form; this is equally true with any construction.

FIGURE 7

Marma Points and Diagonals on the Vastu Purusha Mandala

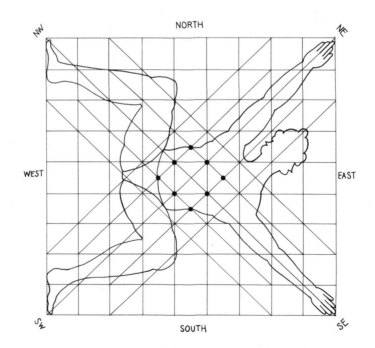

14 Ibid.

The vastu purusha mandala is further divided into a grid of equal squares or *padas*, which are allocated to the appropriate Vedic god, who watches over this specific area of the diagram. Again, the human form is utilized: a pada is about the size of a man's foot. The number of padas inside a vastu purusha mandala may vary from a single pada that would be used to create the blueprint for the Vedic altar to over one thousand padas to create the blueprint for a city. But Brahma always occupies the center of the mandala, sitting on top of vastu purusha's navel, and the orientation of the deities never changes when they appear on a diagram. The actual presence of all the deities or the amount of space allocated to a deity can vary, however, depending on an increase or decrease in the size of the mandala and the number of padas used in the mandala's creation.

ORDER VS. CHAOS

The order and harmony that govern the particular mandala used to develop a site or construct a building is in direct opposition with the disorder and absence of unity that exists outside the mandala. Beyond the mandala is the realm of chaos. Demons with large fangs, frightening eyes, and disheveled hair are said to live beyond the corners of the intermediate directions and formless gods supposedly float beyond the borders of each cardinal direction.

THE VEDIC DEITIES

Forty-five deities including Brahma hold vastu purusha to the ground. According to the English translation of *Architecture of Manasara*, their names are: Isa, Parjanya, Jayanta, Mahendra, Bhanu, Satya, Bhrisa, Antariksha, Agni, Pushan, Vitatha, Griha-kshata, Yama, Gandharva, Bhringa-raja, Mrisa, Pitri, Dauvarika, Sugriva, Pushpadanta, Varuna, Asura, Sosha, Roga, Vayu, Naga, Mukhya, Bhallata, Soma, Mriga, Aditi, Udita, Apavatsya, Apavatsa,

Aryaman, Savitra, Savitra, Vivasvat, Indra, Indrajaya, Mitra, Rudra, Rudrajaya, and Bhudhara.[15]

NORTH

FIGURE 8

Diagram of the Deities for 81 Squares[16]

WEST   EAST

SOUTH

The diagram shows an 81-square grid with deity names: VAYU, NAGA, MUKHYA, BHALLATA, SOMA, MRIGA, ADITI, UDITA, ISA, ROGA, RUDRA, RUDRAJAYA, BHUDHARA, APAVATSA, APAVATSYA, PARJANYA, SOSHA, JAYANTA, ASURA, MITRA, BRAHMA, ARYAMAN, MAHENDRA, VARUNA, ADITYA, PUSHPA-DANTA, SATYA, SUGRIVA, INDRAJAYA, INDRA, VIVASVAT, SAVITRA, SAVITRA, BHRISA, DAUVARIKA, ANTA-RIKSHA, PITRI, MRISA, BHRINGA-RAJA, GANDHARVA, YAMA, GRIHA-KSHATA, VITATHA, PUSHAN, AGNI.

You don't need to know the names of all these deities. In fact, the vastu and Vedic texts often have different spellings of many of the names, and some texts even identify a deity by another name. There is a kernel of truth in Mark Twain's *Following the Equator*:

Indeed, [India] is a country that runs richly to name. The great god Vishnu has 108—108 special ones—108 peculiarly holy ones—names just for Sunday

[15] Prasanna Kumar Acharya, ed. and trans. *Architecture of Manasara: Illustrations of Architectural and Sculptural Objects, Manasara Series: Vol. V* (New Delhi: Munshiram Manoharlal Publishers Pvt. Ltd., 1994).
[16] Ibid.

use only. I learned the whole of Vishnu's 108 by heart once, but they would-
n't stay; I don't remember any of them now but John W.[17]

During Hinduism's long process of evolution, many of the Vedic deities
connected to the vastu purusha mandala also receded into the background
or were absorbed into the huge catalogue of new deities that are worshipped
today. But some of the Vedic deities are still important in vastu: Lord
Brahma, for one, who is considered the creative force in the Hindu trinity,
and the deities known as the guardian deities. Brahma and four of the
guardian deities are connected to the five basic elements, and it is important
to understand how each of them "fits" into the vastu purusha mandala.

THE FIVE ELEMENTS

WATER

The element of water is in the northeast corner of the mandala, along with
the Vedic deity Isa. In the course of the evolution of Hinduism, Isa became
Rudra and much later became Shiva, the destructive force in the Hindu trinity. Spiritually, northeast, an intermediate direction, is considered the gateway
to the gods—a belief reinforced by a myth about Shiva, the god of destruction, and the Goddess Ganga. In this story, Brahma asked the river goddess to
leave her heavenly abode and come down to earth where a king had begged
for her presence. The goddess, who was reluctant to leave, decided that when
she obeyed Brahma's order, she would descend in a heavy deluge.

Shiva caught her torrential waters in his long matted hair, which entan-
gled the goddess and separated her into seven separate streams. One of
them is known as India's sacred Ganges River, which runs from the north to

---

[17] Mark Twain, *Following the Equator, Vol. 11* (New Jersey: The Ecco Press, no date)

the east of India. Many vastu experts, including my teacher Sudesh, say that they frequently find the purest water in the northeast quadrant of a plot.

The northeast, considered the source of positive power from the gods, is also believed to be the source of positive cosmic energy. This theory is based on the fact that as the earth revolves around the sun, the imaginary north-south axis of the earth is not perpendicular with the sun. The earth's axis tilts 23¼ degrees away from due north. Vastu believes that this tilt, which leads to temperature changes and the seasonal variation in the length of day and night, draws in a wide range of cosmic energy through the northeast direction. From the northeast, these energies flow in a southwesterly direction across the site.

FIGURE 9

Rotation of the Earth Around the Sun

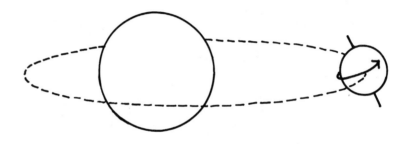

In vastu, the northeastern part of a property is perfect for a pond, a swimming pool, a fountain, or just an open lawn. If this quadrant is lower than the rest of the site, consider yourself lucky. The depression becomes a receptacle that increases the collection of these beneficial energies, which are then channeled through the site. Inside the house, the northeast is ideal for a quiet room for meditation or study. In the northeast of a room place a contemplative object—an image of something or a picture of a living person whom you love or revere.

FIRE

The southeast corner belongs to the element of fire and to Agni, the Vedic god of fire. Agni, called the light of knowledge, also represents the awakening of the soul. In Hinduism, the dead are cremated. As part of the sacrifice, the family member who carries the flaming torch around the funeral pyre finally lights the head of the deceased to permit the liberation of the soul. Thus, fire is the element that is used to free the soul from its entrapment within the body. Fire is used in most important Hindu ceremonies, from rituals in the temple that honor the temple deity to those rituals performed at the important moments in a human's life from birth through death.

The element of fire is extremely delicate and must be handled with care. Too much fire in this quadrant can be overwhelming and destructive. Just a brush with fire can create an injury, while the absence of fire can cause severe discomfort. In the modernized interpretation of vastu, fire also relates to electrical equipment.

On a site, anything that is associated with fire or electricity should preferably be located in the southeast quadrant. In the interior of the house, the kitchen is ideally located in the southeast quadrant; and within a room, the southeast corner is a good location for electrical equipment, such as an entertainment system and a computer.

EARTH

The southwest quadrant belongs to the element of earth, which shares this intermediate direction with Pitri, the Vedic god of ancestors. The connection between this deity and element is potent: The remains of all living organisms decompose into the earth after death. From dust, we return to dust. The southwest quadrant is also associated with wisdom. Our ancestors leave behind generations of knowledge and the knowledge that we gather in our lifetime will be passed on to those who follow us. So when we place ourselves in the southwest, we gather strength as the beneficiaries of time-honored insight and wisdom.

The presence of the earth element in this quadrant also translates into heaviness and weight. This part of the site should bear the heaviest load. The southwest is perfect for a rock garden or heavy sculptures. If there is a natural elevation in this part of the property, leave it alone. Its presence is

49

your good fortune. Inside the house, the master bedroom or the living room should be located in the southwest. If you have children sleeping in this part of the house, this location can make them overbearing and they may try to dominate. The heaviest and largest pieces of furniture should also be in the southwestern part of each room. In general, this quadrant should serve as a barrier to hold in the spiritual forces and positive energy that move from the northeast through the site, the house, and each room to the southwest.

AIR

The element of air, the sustaining breath of all life forms, is in the northwest quadrant. This intermediate direction is also the realm of Vayu, the Vedic god of winds. His presence signifies movement. Vayu helps "move" the thoughts that lead to accomplishment and success.

This identification with movement makes the northwest the most suitable space for a guest bedroom. Your guests won't overstay their welcome. They will instinctively move on. If you watch too much television, make an exception and, instead of placing the television in the southeast corner of a room, put the television set in the northwest. This location, involved with movement, will insure that you grow restless. After a while, you will get up and leave.

SPACE

Brahma, the Creator, reigns from the center, where He shares his holy area, called the Brahmasthana or the place of God, with the element of space. The Brahmasthana is a repository for spiritual energy, which collects here and then radiates outward in the form of beneficial vibrations in every possible direction. Just as the deity in the inner sanctum of a Hindu temple sends out positive vibrations and renewing energies to the devout who come to worship, the presence of Brahma in the center of a secular space sends out vibrations that reenergize and give positive feelings to all who are present.

Since many of the vulnerable points, or *marmas*, of the vastu purusha are inside or near the Brahmasthana, try to keep this part of the building open or at least restrict construction to a minimum in this area. An open center reduces the possibility of hurting the cosmic spirit and also permits the free flow of spiritual vibrations throughout the entire building. The principle of an open center or Brahmasthana should also be mirrored in each room so that the spiritual energies can collect and radiate out vibrations into each individual space as well, thereby creating the same beneficial effect.

IF AN ELEMENT is introduced into a space belonging to another element, and there is no reasonable way to undo the problem, the harmony between the two elements will be disturbed. For example, water may be dominant in a space belonging to fire. Often this is unavoidable. (We rarely have the option of changing the location of our kitchen or bathroom, for instance, unless we are designing our homes from scratch.) To restore the harmony between the two elements, you can make an appeasement: introduce a calming deity, a symbol of the deity, or a prescribed combination of colors to restore the harmony. This, in turn, shows respect to the trespassing element and to the element that presides over the violated space.

THE CARDINAL DIRECTIONS

The cardinal directions—north, south, east, west—also play an important role in vastu and are factored into the construction and interior design of all buildings. The cardinal directions and their significance reveal the importance of balance, not just in the physical world but in the world of moral order. Good and bad. Light and dark. Sunrise and sunset. Enlightenment and ignorance.

Countless dualities exist in our world and their presence serves an important purpose. To understand this, think about how we would appreciate the joy of light without experiencing darkness? How would we respect enlightenment without knowing the frustration of ignorance? We compare sweet with sour, hot with cold, sickness with health, left with right, up with down, youth with old age, pleasure with pain, laughter with tears.

The cardinal directions in the vastu purusha mandala express this principle of dualities. In the construction of a Hindu temple, once we arrive at the inner sanctum, which houses the sacred manifestation of the deity or its symbol, we arrive at that point where we are no longer in the world of duality. We are now in the realm of pure essence.

THE NORTH

Kuber, the god of wealth and indulgence, reigns in the north along with the gods of birth. Kuber shares his realm with Soma, the lord of the moon and the lord of health. As the moon traverses from the northwest to the northeast, it shines in its most heavenly glory. Many healing herbs also thrive in the north, especially in the mountains. In the *Ramayana*, the great Hindu epic, when Lord Rama needed a medicinal herb, he sent the monkey god, Hanuman, north to the Himalayas to bring back the special herb. Hanuman was unable to identify the plant so he brought Lord Rama an entire peak. By keeping therapeutic products and medicines in the northern area of a space, we protect their healing properties. If you are looking for success, try facing north. You will receive the blessings of Kuber and Soma, health and wealth—and this includes spiritual wealth.

THE SOUTH

In the south, we find Yama, the Vedic god of death who also oversees the world of ancestors. Yama passes judgment over the soul and decides its fate at the time of death. Should the soul return to the earth for another round in the cycle of birth and death, or be liberated to find its eternal bliss with the Supreme Creator? And how does the presence of these particular dualities influence us? If you want to put off your moment with Yama (death), you will pay attention to your well-being and Soma (health). If you want to be rewarded at death (Yama), you will think twice about overindulgence (Kuber). In the home or workspace, if you sit with your back to the south you will be reminded of your responsibilities and receive the strength and wisdom of your ancestors.

THE EAST AND WEST

Surya, the Vedic sun god, rules over the east and provides us with light and enlightenment. If the world existed in perpetual darkness, no living organism could survive. By facing east when you study or do creative work, the enlightenment that comes from this direction will inspire you. Varuna, a Vedic deity who has had many different roles and titles over time, is the god of the oceans and rules over the west. From this realm, Varuna lords over the unknown and darkness. It is here that the rays of the sun come to rest, giving way to the darkness of night. Varuna is the duality or opposing principle of Surya. By turning your back on darkness and the unknown, you can receive the light of the east and enlightenment.

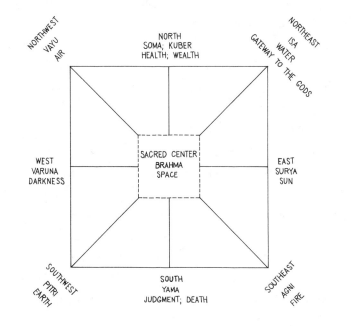

FIGURE 10

Vastu Purusha Mandala with Elements and Cardinal Deities

THE EARTH'S DAILY ROTATION

The deities that reside on the four sides of the border of the vastu purusha mandala play a specific role in the earth's daily rotation. The gods residing on the border from the northeast to the southwest bring light to our world—a light that alters during the course of each day. The gods residing on the borders from the southwest to the northeast carry our world through its period of darkness. Each deity on the border reflects a distinct aspect of the solar and lunar course, which regulates so much of our earthly existence. These deities also remind us of the cycles related to time, which control our existence and the existence of the universe itself.

THE GIFT OF RHYTHM

The dualities and the placement of the deities and elements on the vastu purusha mandala also convey the importance of rhythm in vastu. The division and intended use of the squares in the design process accentuate the concept of rhythm: rhythm that is aesthetically pleasing to the eye; rhythm that symbolically reinforces the physical realities of the universe—time, the day, the seasons, the ongoing principles of the cosmos. They are all examples of rhythm.

Rhythm reinforces the philosophy of the Vedic texts and specifically the theory that is attached to the endless cycles of creation, preservation, and finally destruction, which allows for the creative process to begin again. All matter is bound by a beginning and absolute end to its physical existence. It is part of a rhythmical process that cannot be altered.

To create rhythm in any of the arts, including architecture, requires an understanding of order and proportion. The practice of vastu calls upon an ancient system that uses measures such as the tala (the size of a typical human palm or face), the pada (the length of a typical adult foot), the angula (the thickness of the first joint of the adult middle finger). Measurement, order, and proportion also exist in the vastu purusha mandala. Like music, a three-dimensional structure that is constructed based on mathematically guided proportions establishes rhythm. In architecture, we feel the "music" of the building through a kind of visual rhythm. This rhythm moves our gaze vertically to the top of the structure; horizontal panels create a shift in the rhythm that leads us to look left and right. The end result is dynamic and suggests movement when there is no movement.

OFFERINGS TO THE GODS

Just as the vastu purusha mandala serves as a spiritual blueprint for the best construction of a site, the presence of the deities on the vastu purusha mandala acts as a reminder to the architect, and ultimately to the occupants of the building, that this chosen site, which is a part of the earth, is sacred. It must be revered. This is another reason why every significant step, from the choice of site right down to the completion of the building and the initial step across the threshold by the new occupants, is sanctified by ritual.

The moment in the process when a site has been excavated and it is time to begin the construction of the building's foundation is rich with meaning. The foundation is, after all, the base on which the building will rest—if it is designed according to the sacred vastu purusha mandala, it is nothing less than sanctified ground. This critical point in the construction requires the blessings of the gods.

Any architect trained in vastu understands that the construction process and the presence of a new building on a site can disturb the natural vibrations that once existed there. The architect knows that he must appease the deities and acknowledge the importance of maintaining the Vedic law of nature. As Sudesh explains, even the recitation of mantras that accompany a ritual offering follow a pattern of intonation predetermined to incite the blessings of the gods, so that the gods will keep the positive vibrations in motion.

According to the ancient treatise *Mayamata*, the ritual that occurred before the commencement of the construction of a building's foundation required an offering of a variety of flawless objects that were placed into the excavated site. These offerings included an array of soils—even the soil from an anthill. There were gifts of specific grains and roots. A copper container was placed in the pit and filled with silver, copper, or gold icons of important deities, precious stones—a ruby, a diamond, a sapphire, an emerald—and many semi-precious stones from a tiger's eye to a piece of coral.[18]

There was nothing random about this list of offerings. The offerings connected the site and the act of construction to the philosophy of the Vedic texts and vastu. Earth is offered back to the site—earth of a very particular variety that signifies the five elements that are used to create the universe. The seeds and roots also represent germination and the birth of a new building that will take shape on this site. The gifts of flawless gems and stones are wealth from the earth given back to the earth, wealth that is suitable for the deities who are honored during this important occasion along with the sacred laws that they represent—laws of order and harmony and rhythm and balance.

Today, most of these rituals are only practiced for the construction of a temple. Just a few of the ancient rituals are followed during the construction of secular buildings. The original methods for testing the quality of the soil and water have also been modernized. But their original importance in vastu reinforced the sophisticated and inseparable mix of spirituality and science that define vastu, the Vedic texts, and Hinduism. Their comingling acknowledges the important relationship that exists between the cosmic forces and the five elements and their role in creating harmony or discord within us and within our surroundings.

The performance of the rituals accentuated the connection that exists between the architect and the Supreme Creator, and the connection that exists between the former occupants of the land, known or unknown, and the new occupants of the land. Use and reuse of land or a habitat—creation, destruction, and recreation—reflect the rhythmic continuum that goes on and on as part of the perfect grand plan of the Supreme Creator that is defined not only in vastu but in all the sacred Vedic texts.

---

[18] Kapila Vatsyayan, general ed. and Bruno Dagens, trans., *Mayamata Vol. 1* (Delhi: Indira Gandhi National Centre for the Arts in association with Motilal Banarsidass Publishers, 1994).

3

VASTU IN ANCIENT TEMPLE DESIGN

Requirements of an Architect

[A] man of quality, he must know how to establish buildings and must be well versed in all the sciences; he must be physically perfect, just, compassionate, disinterested, free from envy, without weakness, handsome, and learned in mathematics; he must know the ancient authors and must be straightforward and master of his senses: he must be able to draw and must know the whole country; he must be generous and not greedy; his health must be good, he must be attentive and free from the seven vices (vices springing from anger and lust), possessor of a well chosen name and persevering; he must have crossed the ocean of the science of architecture.

—*MAYAMATA*, CHAPTER FIVE, VOLUME ONE

VASTU CONSIDERS EVERY temple to be the earth-bound dwelling of God; therefore, the architect's design must reflect the perfect proportions and rhythm that exist in the Creator's own creation—the universe. Every aspect of the temple must speak of harmony and balance. The architect must also design a divine structure so that it accommodates the intense level of spiritual energy that radiates out from the center of the inner sanctum. From the placement of every temple sculpture to the narrow finial on the top, every detail is meant to remind the worshipper of the Truth expressed in the *Upanisads*—Tat Tvam Asi (Thou Art That), we are all a part of the Supreme Creative Force. By meeting these objectives, the temple works to reinforce the rituals of worship that were also designed to reflect the same Vedic philosophy.

KHAJURAHO

One can see a brilliant example of these vastu principles at work in the Indian village of Khajuraho, which was once the Rajput capital and religious center of the Chandella dynasty. The Chandella dynasty controlled a huge tract of territory from the tenth to the twelfth centuries AD. Khajuraho is in the northern part of the Indian state of Madhya Pradesh, about 225 miles (395 km) southeast of the city of Agra, the location of the famous Taj Mahal. At this historic village, architects built at least eighty-five temples of which twenty-five remain. Additional temple mounds, however, were discovered in 1999 and await excavation.

Some of the restored temples, originally constructed at the decline of the Chandella dynasty, are magnificent. The Kandariya Mahadeva temple in particular represents one of the finest monuments in India and expresses the brilliance of vastu. The Kandariya Mahadeva not only overwhelms the eye but reaches deep into the soul.

This group of temples and two other temple clusters are the only reminder of the former kingdom's golden age in Khajuraho. Every inch of exquisite sculpture recalls a time when kings celebrated epic battles, royal births, coronations, deaths—a time when kings were committed to the Hindu philosophy with its body of rituals, a time when kings fulfilled their dharma or duty to God by offering their blessings as patrons for the construction of temples.

HINDUISM'S EVOLUTION

The timing of the creation of these temples coincided with the high mark in Indian architectural development. By this time Hinduism had also gone through its own significant process of evolution. The concept of the Hindu Trinity of Brahma, Shiva, and Vishnu was firmly established, and this ushered in a host of popular gods and goddesses who overshadowed or replaced important Vedic deities.

These gods and deities are sacred heroes, mythic and benevolent. They are said to look after the welfare of mankind and destroy the demons who interfere with the realization of the Truth that leads to liberation. Each deity has its distinct personality, specific attributes, and a lineage that personalizes Hinduism. These gods and goddesses are accessible; worshippers can even choose to focus their worship on the gods of their choice, instead of worshipping all of them. Hinduism introduced freedom into the concept of devotion.

It was always understood, however, that every one of these deities was the embodiment of perfection and represented an aspect of the one Supreme Creator. Each deity, in its own unique manifestation, was ultimately a reminder of the Truth that is revealed in the philosophy of the *Upanisads* and other Vedic texts: Thou Art That.

Temple carvings and sculptures of these deities are abundant in Khajuraho. It is also a place where we see the new relationship between the deities of the Vedic Era and the popular deities still worshipped today. We also see that each representation of a deity follows vastu guidelines to determine its size, proportion, and actual placement on a temple wall or pillar. As is true with the Vedic deities, all the deities that became prominent with the evolution of Hinduism are imbued with symbolism. The following section provides a brief introduction to some of the important deities and their symbols.[19]

---

[19]See Chapter 9, *Appeasing the Gods, Appeasing Your Soul*, for more information on these deities.

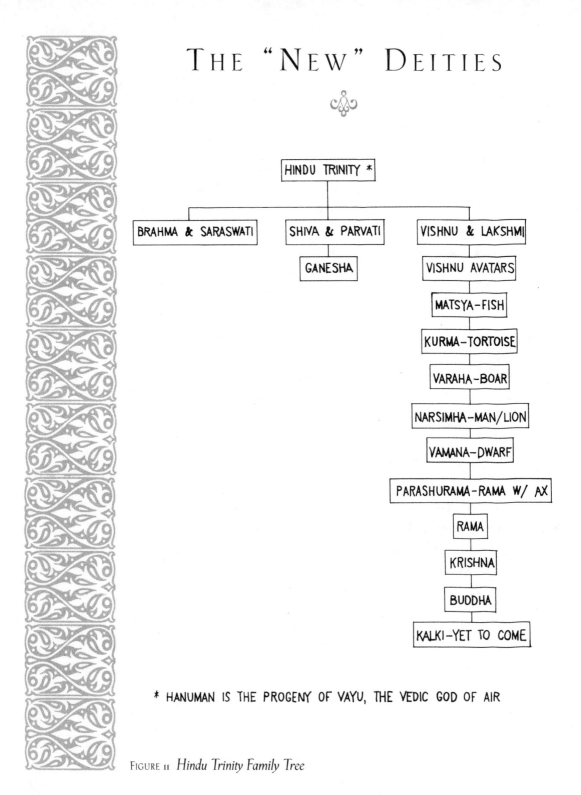

THE "NEW" DEITIES

Figure 11 *Hindu Trinity Family Tree*

FIGURE 12 *Brahma*

Lord of Creation in the Hindu Trinity. Four bearded heads with each face representing one of the *Vedas*, the source of spiritual wisdom. Each hand signifies a cardinal direction and omnipresence. His eyes represent the sun and moon, each nose the life-sustaining breath. His beards are white— a reminder that the act of creation began long, long ago. He often sits on a lotus, the symbol of Truth. His consort is Saraswati, the goddess of wisdom and knowledge.

FIGURE 13 *Saraswati*

Goddess of wisdom and knowledge, she is the embodiment of spiritual wisdom and referred to as the Mother of the *Vedas*. Normally shown with four hands: two hands play the *vina* (stringed instrument) through which she spreads the Word; a third hand holds a *Veda*; a fourth hand holds rosaries signifying need for meditation and chanting. Through acquisition of knowledge and acts of devotion one comes to the Truth.

FIGURE 14 *Shiva*

Lord of Destruction with many manifestations. Also called the Lord of Yoga and often shown in meditation— symbolizing the path to self-realization. His left and right eyes represent the outer world. His third eye represents destruction and therefore rebirth. His throat is blue from holding poison swallowed in a battle with demons. His matted hair carries the sacred River Ganga. The crescent moon hair ornament holds the nectar of immortality. The poison and the nectar symbolize the presence of dualities in our life. The rest of Shiva's body is fair, symbolic of peace. The ashes remind us of the oneness of all matter—everything decomposes to ashes or dust. His consort is the Goddess Parvati who assumes many forms, including Durga.

Figure 15 *Parvati*

Goddess of power and strength who represents the *Shakti* (female power or active energy) of Shiva. A mother goddess who assumes many forms that complement each form of Shiva. Emergence out of the ocean of milk makes her the symbol of purity. She also embodies goodness and represents the ideal woman. Usually shown with Shiva and Ganesha or with all her manifestations, such as Durga.

Figure 16 *Durga*

The wrathful protector and a symbol of power. Durga overcomes evil and demons, including destructive elements that reside within us. Often shown with eight hands. Each hand carries a symbolic weapon to destroy weakness and evil. Usually rides a lion or tiger—symbolic of the subjugation of the ego.

Figure 17 *Ganesha*

The benevolent elephant-headed god—remover of obstacles and god of auspicious beginnings—is the first deity worshipped in Hindu ceremonies. He opens the doors of spiritualism. Ganesha, the son of Shiva and Parvati, represents wisdom and discretion. Always accompanied by an obedient rat, his vehicle. The rat honors Ganesha's commands and subjugates its typical behavior—symbolizing the need to subjugate our own desires to reach the Truth.

Figure 18 *Vishnu*

Lord of preservation and third deity in the Hindu Trinity. The preserver of the universe, Vishnu is filled with mercy and devotion for all creation. Vishnu represents pure consciousness. His blue color symbolizes infinity. Each of four hands carries a sacred object: the lotus, a conch shell that spreads the primordial word AUM; a discus or *chakra* (wheel) that represents the cycle of time; a mace that destroys evil forces that steer us from the right path. Vishnu has nine *avatars* (manifestations), which he sent to earth to defeat evil and protect the law of dharma at various times during the earth's existence. Rama and Krishna are avatars. His consort is Lakshmi, the goddess of wealth.

Figure 19 *Lakshmi*

Consort of Vishnu and goddess of wealth, including a wealth of proper values and spiritual goodness. With each avatar of Vishnu, Lakshmi assumes a different role and name; however, she always represents the Shakti or power that is represented in each avatar. Lakshmi usually stands or sits on a lotus, which is a symbol of knowledge, and connects back to wealth. To acquire wealth, we must first acquire knowledge. Her palm held downward represents a gesture of giving.

Figure 20 *Rama*

Seventh avatar of Vishnu. Represents the importance of detachment from earthly desires. Sent to earth as the son of a king, Rama's duty was to destroy the evil embodied in Ravana, a powerful rival king. Determined to fulfill his dharma, he is also recognized as a symbol of goodness and the embodiment of the ideal man. Wears a string of perfect jewels that signify his perfect attributes. Carries a bow and arrows to conquer challenges within him and in the external world.

Figure 21 *Krishna*

Eighth avatar of Vishnu. Krishna's name means dark, and he symbolizes the emergence of truth out of darkness and the resulting state of bliss. The music of his flute represents the ecstasy that comes with self-realization. Krishna is often depicted in a pose of contentment to signify the consummate joy that comes with the realization of the Truth.

Figure 22 *Hanuman*

The monkey-god who represents wisdom, strength, and devotion to dharma. When Rama asked Hanuman to find medicinal herbs in the Himalayas, the monkey-god brought back an entire mountain. Usually carries a huge mace or club to destroy evil. Often, one hand is held palm upward in a gesture that offers spiritual blessings.

KHAJURAHO TEMPLES

The best way to describe a vastu temple is to take you to Khajuraho to see the Matangesvara Temple, a "living" temple where a priest continues to perform pujas, and the Kandariya Mahadeva Temple, which is an historic monument and no longer used for worship. In 1999, I visited this village with my friend Toshi. Pockmarked paved roads lead into semi-tropical Khajuraho, where undulating low mountains create a natural rhythm in the distance. The two shrines that we planned to see stand back from the skinny main street that cuts through the center of the village—two special rooks in a group of the temples created by the Chandella dynasty.

MATANGESVARA TEMPLE

The eleventh-century AD Matangesvara Temple overlooks the rectangular Shivasagar Lake, which rests at the bottom of the hill that supports the temple. Most scholars believe that this small temple was originally built as a memorial to a Chandella king. It follows the vastu guidelines for such a structure, with a combined sanctum and hall and a roof designed as a pyramid.

Toshi and I joined a small group of worshippers who had come to the modest shrine to receive blessings from the *linga* (phallus) symbol of Shiva, which is honored inside the small sanctum. Shiva is an extremely popular Hindu deity and most of the significant temples in Khajuraho, including the Kandariya Mahadeva, are dedicated either to him or to Vishnu. In fact, Shiva and Vishnu long ago eclipsed Brahma, the Lord of Creation, in prominence. Very few temples were built to honor Brahma.

We removed our shoes and many of the worshippers pressed either their head or right hand to a lower step on the staircase that led to the temple platform. This is a customary gesture that conveys respect to the deity that is revered within the shrine. Midway up the steps to the small Matangesvara

64

Temple, we stopped briefly to pay our respects to a statue of Ganesha, the elephant-headed god and remover of obstacles. A blur of right hands brushed the granite surface of the stone image of this unusual yet most beloved deity who is invoked at the start of any new undertaking.

We continued up the remaining steps to the porch entrance of the shrine. One by one, worshippers rang the bell that hung in the entrance to announce our arrival to the deity and to ward away any lingering evil spirits. This act also reminds us to turn our thoughts away from the external world and focus on the inner self so that we are prepared to worship the deity honored within.

A young priest in long shirt and *dhoti* (long wrap around the lower half of the body) was sitting on an elevated platform next to an enormous 8½-foot-high sandstone linga, which was placed in the direct center of the small shrine.

The Shiva linga is situated inside a circular receptacle called the *yoni* (female sexual organ), thus connecting it to *Shakti*, or female energy. This connection reinforces the concept of union and the act of creation. The linga represents the male principle and the receptacle is considered female and represents the principle of Shakti.

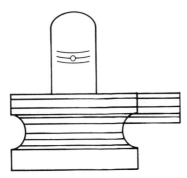

FIGURE 23

Linga and Yoni

The platform with the huge linga takes up almost the entire interior of the sanctuary, leaving just enough room for the narrow ambulatory passage that encircles the simple interior with its minimal carvings, three balconies, and pillars. All these architectural details conform to vastu guidelines.

The Ritual of Worship

Worshippers stood before the linga and offered flowers and rupees (Indian currency) to the officiating priest. These gifts were for the deity who blesses the devout with his own spiritual gifts. As the priest chanted mantras and sprinkled us with holy water, the smell of incense carried through the air and reminded us that the Supreme Essence is everywhere, formless and unseen. The priest blessed each of us with a saffron *tikka* mark placed on the forehead at the location of the third eye—the eye of wisdom.

The actions of the priest and the devout offered respect not just to Shiva, but to the five elements that exist here and everywhere. Water flows out of the yoni that supports the linga. The smell of earth mingles with the fragrance of burning camphor, a gummy compound that has been reduced to liquid; this reduction to liquid stands for the need to dissolve the false importance of the ego to reach the Truth. Spiritual energy floats throughout the entire space.

Standing within this temple, I found I had no urge whatsoever to leave. I was caught up in a feeling of inner joy. I was especially conscious of the importance of fire, the element of sacrifice, which manifested here in the burning camphor oil that floats inside the brass platter near the priest. The flame of this burning oil represents the fire of knowledge and the burning of the barriers that exist within us and keep us from realizing that our atma (or soul) is part of the Paramaatma or Supreme Essence. While the priest chanted, he held out the platter to each of us. My right hand rotated above the delicate fire. Then I put my hand in front of my eyes in an act that expresses the wish to absorb the Truth of the Lord that is revealed in the power of the flame.

KANDARIYA MAHADEVA

After Toshi and I left the Matangesvara, we met a senior government guide, Brijendra Singh, who was going to tell us about the effect of vastu on the Kandariya Mahadeva, which was also built in the eleventh century AD.

Brijendra steered us onto a manicured lawn to a vantage point about 200 feet from the temple. From here, we discussed the concept of the four concentric zones that are so clearly expressed in the layout of the temple site and its interior. These zones reflect the intention of the vastu architect to create a design that takes the worshipper from the external world of forms to the formless world—eternity, which comes with the release from the endless cycle of life and death.

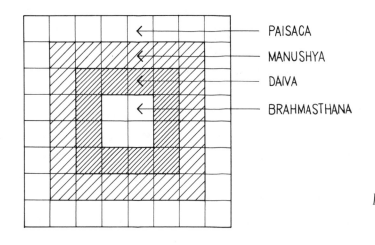

PAISACA

MANUSHYA

DAIVA

BRAHMASTHANA

FIGURE 24

Diagram of
the Zones

The temple site represents the outermost and fourth zone, *paisaca*, which covers the world of objects that define earthly existence. When we step inside the temple, our mind then starts to turn inward so that we can enter the third zone, *manushya*, which represents the state of consciousness. The vastu design of the temple, with an ambulatory passage that draws us closer and closer to the inner sanctum, leads us into the second zone, *daiva*, which signifies the difficult and slow process that finally brings us to the goal of enlightenment. When we reach the inner sanctum, we are in the first and central zone, the Brahmasthana, the source of spiritual power, which emanates from this space through powerful positive vibrations and turns our thoughts to the Divine.

The Symbolism of the Vertical Ascent

This reinforcement of the Vedic philosophy is mirrored in the ascent of the temple. At the base of the temple, the sculptures represent the world of humanity and the daily activities that defined its age of construction: battle

67

scenes and hunts in the jungle, domestic scenes. Directly above this band of carvings is the higher realm of demigods, celestial musicians and angels, and *mithunas* (erotic couples) who express in accessible human symbolism the belief of the union of the atma or soul with the Paramaatma, or Supreme Soul.

Moving higher up the temple, we come to the mass of eighty-four *shikharas* (spires or peaks) that jut up from the temple and create the roof. These shikharas are decorated primarily with geometric patterns. Within this entire mass of vertical projections just an occasional deity is showcased in a niche or corner projection. This is the world of Essence, Truth, and Cosmic Energy that is invisible yet present everywhere. The temple shikharas remind us that we must get beyond the limitations of our own body and its demands and distractions so that we can discover the divinity that exists within us. The lack of earthly forms on the spires takes us from the realm of manifestations into the realm of the invisible Supreme Essence.

The gold finial on the summit is placed inside a receptacle, which is called the *kalasha*. The celestial architect, Vishwakarma, originally created the kalasha to hold *amrit* (the nectar that brings *moksha* or immortality). The kalasha and finial represent the Supreme Essence in its unseen form. The worshipper can see this part of the temple from a distance and knows that the journey made through the temple is symbolic. It is a journey intended to remind the worshipper of the proper path to follow, right now in this current life, in order to reach the nectar of immortality (moksha).

When worshippers arrive at the temple, they go inside and pray before the image or symbol of the deity. While they pray to the deity, they know that the deity is symbolic of something that is formless and unseen. The function of the form is similar to the function of a myth: it is filled with deeper meanings that are presented at a level that all worshippers can appreciate. They know that the linga stands for the Supreme Essence, which cannot be touched or viewed with the eyes.

Presence of Dualities

From outside the temple, we are also reminded of the important principle of dualities through the architect's design. From any angle, we notice the beautiful projection of balconies with their elaborate ornamentation. Depending on the location of the sun, the balconies shimmer or are bathed in a soft luster, and they throw shadows that create a play of light and dark on the exquisite carvings chiseled into the exterior walls. This ongoing expression of light and dark created by the balconies is a constant reminder of the presence of dualities—an important concept in the Vedic philosophy.

The Creation of Rhythm and Balance

FIGURE 25

Exterior of the Kandariya Mahadeva

Rhythm, so important in the vastu guidelines, is built into every bit of the Kandariya Mahadeva. "Vertical rhythm and horizontal rhythm," said Brijendra, "that's what makes a building sing." The rhythm, he explained, was factored into the design by following the vastu guidelines for appropriate proportions. All the sculptures, with their well-defined proportions, break up the surface so that every level draws our attention. And within the images of the deities, their pose, their attributes, their position on a frieze, and their placement with another deity convey important messages involving enlightenment and immortality.

69

Balconies are built into three sides of the temple. The perfect alignment and size of the balconies creates balance and harmony—a balance that is matched by the majestic design of the forward projections of the portico-styled entrance. There is nothing jarring about the aesthetics of this temple. It reflects the brilliance of the vastu guidelines, which the architects complemented with their stupendous talent.

Rhythm of the Shikharas

The Kandariya Mahadeva, which sits on a wide platform, has five sections that are joined together. The individual roofs on the *mukha-mandapa* (entrance portico), the *mandapa* (initial compartment), and the *maha-mandapa* (enclosed hall) are each constructed in a pyramidal shape that includes a cluster of ascending and descending peaks. The roofs on the next two sections, the *antarala* (vestibule) and the sacred *garbhagriha* (womb chamber) or inner sanctum, are shikharas, with a mass of rounded spires that continue the upward thrust and reinforce the rising and descending principle that is seen in mountains.

Not only is there an accumulation of rising peaks, but the rising peaks on each roof are also subtly and slowly inclined toward the highest spire. The cumulative effect of this rhythmic design brings all the peaks together to create a superb lyricism—music frozen into form. The soaring effect of these eighty-four peaks, graduating upward to the crowning gold finial atop the highest spire, also create such a sense of verticality that it makes the temple seem much taller than its 110 feet (which includes the height of the platform base).

Another feeling of rhythm is accentuated in the horizontal bands of carvings that go around the entire temple. They bind together each roof and each part of the temple so that the structure is cohesive, visually and philosophically. The horizontal bands reinforce the "oneness" of this perfect three-dimensional form—the oneness between us and That.

A visit to a temple constructed according to the vastu purusha mandala reminds us every step of the way that we are on a path to the ultimate goal.

Each new area helps us prepare for the symbol of Shiva contained inside the sacred garbhagriha (womb chamber). Stepping before Shiva's symbol is our ultimate destination, philosophically and symbolically. One does not just walk through a vastu temple; one takes a symbolic journey through the stages that remind us of the Truth.

The Temple Platform

The Kandariya Mahadeva is built on an extremely spacious ten-foot high platform or *jagati* that resembles a terrace. Many scholars believe that four small shrines once graced each corner of the jagati. The original construction of five structures, while dedicated to particular deities, would have been a reaffirmation of the importance of the five elements of space, air, fire, water, and earth as the source of all creation. The element of space was associated with the ornate temple, built to honor Shiva, which still stands in the center of the platform.

We walked clockwise around the platform of the Kandariya Mahadeva and saw how the vastu architect honors the rituals attached to Hinduism. The first niche on the exterior wall contained a carving of Ganesha, the elephant-headed god, the son of Shiva, and the first deity prayed to in a Hindu ceremony. Brijendra pointed out that the Kandariya Mahadeva was positioned on an east-west axis, with its entrance opening to the east. The east is the direction of knowledge, enlightenment, and most especially spiritual enlightenment. He called our attention to the temple's entrance. It was dark and mysterious, and resembled a cave. The temple's similarity to a mountain and a cave was deliberate.

The Kandariya Mahadeva is dedicated to Shiva, the deity in the Hindu Trinity who represents the destructive aspect in the process of creation, preservation, and destruction. The destructive aspect of Shiva is necessary. It allows for the ongoing process of re-creation, which sustains the universe. The undulating shikharas on the Kandariya Mahadeva, moving along a gradual ascent to the summit, remind us of the path that leads to freedom from the cycle of life and death into the realm of pure essence and immortality.

The Symbolism of the Mountain and Cave

Shiva's abode is in the mountains—the great Himalayan Mountains—and specifically Mount Kailash, which is believed to be a northern extension of the very sacred Mount Meru, celestial home of Indra, the most important Vedic deity. Mount Meru, the Mount Olympus of the Hindus, contains the cities of the gods and celestial spirits.

In Hindu mythology, Mount Meru is said to be at the center or navel of the earth, its spiritual axis, with every part of the universe pivoting around it. This same mountain is also sacred to Buddhists and figures prominently in a similar context within their own spiritual mythology. The Himalayas are also the source of the sacred River Ganges, one of the seven rivers created by Shiva out of the Goddess Ganga, which traverses down the mountains to the plains and heads east through the holy city of Varanasi.

But Shiva doesn't just live on Mount Kailash. He and his consort Parvati live within the darkness of a cave contained inside the holy peak. Many of India's earliest temples were dug into mountains, the temple caves of Badami in the southern state of Karnataka and the Ellora and Ajanta caves in the state of Maharastra. Caves also serve as the cavernous retreats for many swamis and yogis who choose to do penance or meditate in silence and solitude for long stretches of time in a dark enclosed space that is replete with potency. In Hinduism, caves are considered sacred; they are symbols of the womb and the womb's importance as a creative force. To meditate inside a cave leads to a form of rebirth and renewal.

The garbhagriha found in most Hindu temples are purposely small, square (to reflect the perfect universe) and dark. Natural light is blocked out and the inner sanctum walls are adorned with very little or no sculpture to accentuate the austere massiveness of a cavelike recess. This is certainly true for the garbhagriha inside the Kandariya Mahadeva.

The Temple Interior

As we walked through the portico of the temple and into the main chamber, Brijendra, who must have entered this temple with tourists a thousand times in his life, still sighed: "Isn't it lovely? Look at the contrasts. You can see everything and just with natural light."

The interior is haunting in its beauty—a beauty enhanced by an abundance of over 200 temple carvings. Light, which flows into the small temple from the balconies and entrance, casts rays onto some of the slender pillars and unusually elongated shapes of female figures that speak of verticality and ascendancy. In other areas the light is intermittent, and not strong.

The temple's interior reveals more balance and harmony. Some of this is created by the ongoing dance of light and dark. Some of it is expressed through the presence of the guardian deities of the cardinal directions who remind us, again, of dualities: good and bad, life and death, enlightenment and ignorance. We are also reminded of balance and harmony through the important five elements, which are honored through their representative Vedic deities placed at the location assigned to them on the vastu purusha mandala.

A carving of Agni, the fire element, is in the southeast. Pitri, the earth element, is in the southwest. Vayu, the element of air, is in the northwest. Isa, the water element, is in the northeast. The Shiva-linga, resting in the inner sanctum or Brahmasthana, represents the element of space. And if Kandariya Mahadeva were a "living" temple instead of an historic monument, we would see all these same elements expressed during the performance of every puja.

FIGURE 26

Diagram of Temple Interior

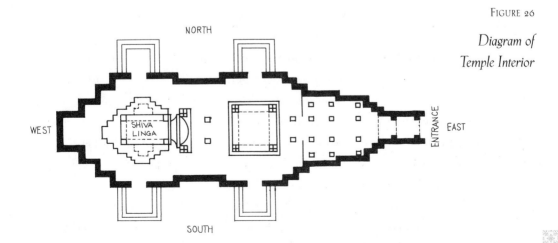

Brijendra echoed the words of Sudesh when he said that the circumambulation around the exterior of the inner sanctum is a conscious effort, achieved through the vastu guidelines, that prepares the mind for the representation of the deity inside the garbhagriha, the most hallowed part of the shrine. The vastu architect wanted the worshipper to discard all feelings of conflict so that the mind can receive the positive vibrations emanating from all the sculpted gods. All tangible boundaries, such as the temple walls, and all intangible boundaries, such as mental and emotional thoughts held within an individual, were to be discarded, melted away from the mind.

The vastu guidelines had also led to the creation of a religious structure that drew upon the spiritual symbols attached to the cave. The architect made worshippers consciously aware of their movement from an area within the temple, marked by intermittent light and abundant carvings, to a small area—the garbhagriha—where darkness and simple purity prevailed.

Circumambulation

As worshippers circumambulate the interior, they are expected to stop periodically and meditate before carvings of important deities that are stationed on the interior walls. Studying the deities and the profound meanings connected to them puts visitors into a position of grace and awe, which prepares them for the most powerful vibrations, projecting off the representation of the sacred deity that awaits inside the inner sanctum.

As I looked at these temple deities, the mood in the eyes of each carving always drew me forward to examine it more closely. Sometimes the eyes were closed in deep meditation; sometimes they were open and serene, or they were commanding, or they were completely preoccupied with an accompanying deity. I saw how vastu used the placement and proportion of a deity to create visual power: So many times the eyes of the deities intentionally meet the eyes of the viewer. In one arrangement of carvings, their size reflected their importance in the temple: Shiva was placed in the center niche. Above this manifestation of Shiva was another niche containing a carving of Vishnu smaller than the carving of Shiva. Brahma was in a niche directly below Shiva, and was the smallest of the three deities.

Interior Ascent

The pillars and the deities stacked in vertical rows also accentuated the importance of the ascent, as did the walk through the temple. As we proceeded from one chamber to the next, we climbed steps that led to a higher floor, until the last few steps brought us to the garbhagriha. Here, too, the verticality continued. The most sacred object in the temple, the marble Shiva Linga, was placed on a yoni pedestal that elevated the symbol of this deity so that it rose above the highest floor in the temple, the floor of the garbhagriha.

Garbhagriha

As I stood before the garbhagriha, my mind was completely focused. I was ready to view the symbol of the deity inside this central sanctum, which was only ten feet square, with walls that were nearly completely unadorned. I noticed a beautiful carved panel in the lintel over the door that led into the holy sanctuary. Shiva occupied the center position, flanked by Vishnu and Brahma—another architectural clue that identified the god honored in this temple.

The connection of the cave and mountain further accentuate vertical movement. The shaft of the Shiva Linga is in the exact center of the womb, which is also the Brahmasthana. The Shiva Linga also sits at the highest point inside the temple. The shaft, which is four feet in circumference, is the spiritual axis that connects to the gold finial on top of the highest peak on the temple roof, which is directly above the garbhagriha. The linga's energy travels up the temple axis to the top of the finial, which is the highest point of the building. There, the energy continues to radiate and merge with the invisible Essence, symbolized by the linga. The verticality connected to the Shiva Linga shaft speaks of the same Ultimate Truth. By praying before the Shiva Linga in its womb chamber, the devout experience a symbolic return to the womb and an act of renewal and rebirth.

The path to immortality is also echoed on the horizontal plane. We walk from a large open space marked by its dualities—light and dark—and the dualities attached to the cardinal deities—to the garbhagriha, which is an absolute contrast—small, square, affording minimal visibility and near barren of all carvings. Our eyes are meant to focus on the Shiva Linga and the message it conveys: We have entered a realm where the dualities cease to exist. We have entered the realm of pure essence that exists beyond the world of time and the cycles of life and death.

Ultimately the entire temple speaks of symbolism. The cave is deep inside the mountain, under the highest peak. The connection is with Mount Meru, where the Shiva Linga reinforces the all-important spiritual axis. The garbhagriha or womb chamber translates into a Brahmasthana that sends out immense spiritual power.

The vastu guidelines, which are used in the creation of the temple, accentuate the Vedic philosophy. The viewer who stands before the garbhagriha is filled with nothing less than reverence. After all, few symbols can be as potent as the womb. It is from the womb that life defines itself. It is in the womb that the merged forces of the male and female union create the new essence with its distinct form and its own vital force of energy. It is in the womb, as in this temple chamber, that all the five elements have their role and importance in the manifestation of life.

It is from the womb of the temple that the spiritual energy of the form radiates outward and beyond its essence. We feel it and it fills us with its spiritual energy, reminding us of our connection to the Supreme Essence symbolized by the Shiva Linga, which carries our thoughts up to the highest kalasha and finial that hold the nectar of immortality. This is the aim of earthly existence and this aim is mirrored in all religions. "The amrit of immortality is the most difficult goal to reach," Sudesh would say whenever we talked about vastu and temple architecture.

BADRINATH TEMPLE

At one of my meetings with Sudesh, I had tried to get him to talk about a new temple complex that was in a state of perpetual construction on the outskirts of Delhi. The ongoing construction of the site dripped with a lavishness provided by donations from India's wealthy elite. I wanted to know if what I had heard was true: that these shrines were not being built according to vastu. Sudesh waved his hand at me as if to shoo away my question and responded that he did not know. "It's the ancient temples," he said, "that take your breath away."

Sudesh and I did discuss incredible events that surrounded the recent history of a vastu-designed Hindu temple that has been renovated over the centuries and even existed for a while as a Buddhist shrine. The Badrinath shrine rests in an ethereal setting, nestled in a high mountain valley in the Himalayas. A tourist brochure says of the old shrine, which is the holiest of four sacred shrines in this mountain range: "There are many sacred spots of pilgrimage in the heavens, earth and nether world, but there has been none equal to Badri, nor shall there be."[20]

The Badrinath Temple is dedicated to the Hindu deity Vishnu, who, legend says, was punished and forced to sit in meditation in this spot in the valley after he permitted Lakshmi, his consort, to commit the indiscretion of massaging his feet. The meditative pose of the black stone representation of Vishnu recalls the Buddha, which is not a coincidence. The Buddha is the ninth avatar or incarnation of Vishnu. This also explains why this Hindu shrine was converted temporarily into a Buddhist shrine.

Throngs of Hindu devout pay homage to Vishnu at this extraordinarily sacred shrine. While the temple now has colorfully painted exterior walls, its garbhagriha, which has never been modified since its original construction thousands of years ago, is humble in comparison to the ornately carved Kandariya Mahadeva in Khajuraho. This is probably intentional. The temple site in a valley, which is 3,133 meters (10,276 feet) above sea level, is so spectacular that the modest shrine has a splendor that sets it apart from and above many other man-made creations.

The Badrinath Temple also rests in an earthquake belt. In 1991 a quake measuring 6.8 on the Richter scale rattled through this part of the

20 *Uttar Pradesh: A to Z* (Lucknow: Uttar Pradesh Department of Tourism, undated).

Himalayas, causing trees, earth, and boulders to break loose from mountains, leveling entire villages. Roadbeds disappeared and rivers shifted course. Rockslides tumbled down on both sides of the Badrinath, but the temple, with its precious inner sanctum, was unscathed.

When I suggested to Sudesh that this was some sort of miracle, he agreed. But he also said that vastu's guidelines did teach temple architects how to examine stones, rocks, all the aspects of a potential construction site. "They understood fault lines," said Sudesh. "They noticed how the sheep grazed— where they went and where they wouldn't go. They examined the stones and saw what had happened to them over the ages." Vastu showed architects how to read nature's legends. The architects had paid attention and the Badrinath Temple survived.

❈ 4 ❈

VASTU AND THE VEDIC VIEW OF HEALTH

An average individual believes in refinement, in becoming finer and
finer. He is like an artist who wants to improve the quality of his life
and to be better than he is. The yogi, too, knows that he has to refine
himself more and more. He accepts death happily and believes in
rebirth as he strives to be finer and finer in his way of thinking and
acting. When seeds are sown, the plants come up, and when the
plants are mature they give new seeds to sow for the next crop and
the next harvest. Thus the yogi develops the quality of his life so that
a good seed may emerge, and his next life may bring the harvest of
spiritual fragrance.

—B. K. S. IYENGAR, *THE TREE OF YOGA*

THE SCIENCE OF vastu is a glove around the hand of its sister sciences, ayurveda and yoga. All three are both spiritual and scientific, and all three are rooted in Vedic philosophy, drawing their logic from the Vedic theory of the creation of the universe and the creation of the self. All three sciences recognize the importance of a harmonious environment and home, a harmonious balance in the body and in the mind. We need harmony to be in a position to work toward enlightenment—the awareness of Tat Tvam Asi (Thou Art That)—part of the indefinable and unseen Supreme Spirit.

If harmony doesn't exist in our home or workspace, the two places where we spend the great majority of our time, our body's own harmony is disturbed and we never experience inner peace. If we can't realize inner peace, we sabotage the benefits that come with ayurveda and yoga. Vastu, as the protective glove, safeguards the environment most conducive to the healthy body and mind so central to ayurveda and yoga.

THE VASTU BODY

Very few people would think of themselves as a living example of architecture. But we are. From the moment of conception, a human form evolves inside the womb. The body, therefore, is a perfect example of vastu. And throughout our lives, our vastu body serves as the primary temple that shelters our soul. This comparison of the body to a temple appears repeatedly in ayurveda and yoga.

Remember, too, that vastu uses the human body as a point of comparison and reference. As I discussed earlier, the human body from the top of the head to the soles of the feet and with arms fully extended to the sides creates an exact square—the shape that represents the perfect cosmos, the shape of the temple inner sanctum, which houses the manifestation of the Supreme Creative Force, just as the body houses the soul whose essence is a part of That.

This inner sanctum, which is also called the garbhagriha or womb chamber, is another example of the weaving of the human body into vastu. And what about the vastu purusha who resides in the vastu purusha mandala and the spirit's marma points, which I mentioned in Chapter 2? Everything related to vastu purusha and his vulnerabilities corresponds to the human body and its physical vulnerabilities—the lungs, kidneys, and heart.

To see how they work in tandem with vastu, it is useful to have at least a rudimentary understanding of ayurveda and yoga.

A BRIEF HISTORY OF AYURVEDA AND YOGA

Both ayurveda and yoga are believed to have been passed on from Brahma to the rishis during the Vedic Age. But the most celebrated compilations on ayurveda and yoga, *Charaka Samhita* and *The Yoga-Sutra of Patanjali*, are of more recent origin—usually dated anywhere from 1500 BC to AD 600. The practice of these sciences, however, most definitely predates each of these texts.

Ayurveda, the science of life, is believed to be the oldest medical system in the world—ironic when you consider that in the West it is often lumped in with so-called New Age practices. Ayurveda, which comes from the *Atharva Veda*, concentrates on disease *prevention* and *rejuvenation* and presents a holistic theory about health. Good health includes a healthy body, mind, and spirit. Ayurveda interprets illness, in many circumstances, as a symptom pointing to an imbalance in the body and in one's lifestyle.

The full science of yoga is not fully understood by many Westerners. Most people think of yoga as a physical activity that concentrates on the performance of body postures combined with breathing exercises that strengthen the body and rid it of impurities. Many people also think that meditation is separate from yoga. They go to a yoga class one day and a meditation class another.

But meditation is a primary part of yoga; and the more physical aspect described above represents only a small part of *ashtanga*, or the classical eight-step yoga. *Yoga* means "union"—union with the Divine. The first two steps in ashtanga cleanse the heart and ensure proper thoughts and actions through self-restraint, to prevent unethical behavior and to establish a commitment to purity and austerity. Steps three through five teach us how to control our body, mind, and senses: step three is the practice of body postures; step four the practice of breathing exercises; step five teaches how to block out the senses so that the mind can turn inward, without distraction. Step six (the practice of concentration) and step seven (the practice of meditation) keep us focused inward and prepare us for the most difficult and final step: the union of the soul with the Paramaatma or Supreme Essence.

There are many other schools of yoga that lead to this same goal:

1. *Hatha yoga*, which is similar to ashtanga but based on a different ancient treatise, *Hatha Yoga Pradipika*. This text emphasizes proper breathing to draw oneself into the self to discover union with the Supreme Essence.
2. *Bhakti yoga* chooses the path of unwavering devotion and pure self-less love offered unconditionally to the Divine. This includes the Divine self that exists in all creation.
3. *Karma yoga* honors the life of selfless actions, which are performed without expectation of reward and in a state of complete detachment. Followers of karma yoga dedicate their life to serving the Supreme Spirit.
4. *Jhana yoga* is the yoga of knowledge. It approaches the goal of union through discrimination and reason. Spiritual growth through wisdom allows the follower of jhana yoga to turn inward and see the Truth.
5. *Raja yoga* is a meditative school of yoga that focuses on the final three steps of ashtanga to realize the final goal.

THE LAWS OF NATURE AND THE LAWS OF THE BODY

Each of these sciences respects the connection between the universe and the self. They all honor the binding connection between the laws and processes that govern the world of nature and the laws and processes that govern the functioning of the human body. In addition to an awareness that all matter, including each one of us, is made up of the five elements—space, air, fire, water, and earth—every object also represents the union of purusha (the unseen essence or energy or spirit) and prakriti (matter). By observing and learning from the laws that govern nature, ayurveda, yoga, and vastu use this knowledge to maintain and improve the well-being of the body, mind, and spirit. That these sciences share this link should not surprise us.

THE IMPORTANCE OF THE FIVE ELEMENTS

Vastu, as we've seen, works to preserve the balance of the five elements. By ensuring that each element is placed in its appropriate location on the property, inside the house, and in each room, the vastu architect seeks to restore the harmony that may have been disrupted by the addition of a new structure, which creates its own energies and vibrations.

Ayurveda and yoga adhere to this same theory. Both sciences believe that—with the exception of external injuries, such as wounds, and congenital diseases that come with birth—all illnesses are a result of an imbalance in the body's original configuration of these same five elements. When the original balance is disturbed, the body is weakened and its natural immune system is compromised.

TRIDOSHAS

Long ago, ayurveda developed a system of *tridoshas* (three metabolic processes that involve the elements inside the body). This system, which is also recognized by yoga, maintains that the doshas control all our bodily processes. Indeed, certain asanas and breathing exercises in yoga specifically benefit a particular dosha. As in vastu, each element, associated with a dosha, has its own characteristics.

Tridoshas

Dosha	Element
Vata	Air with space
Pitta	Fire with water
Kapha	Water with earth

83

VATA

The first dosha is known as *vata*. Vata represents the element of air combined with the element of space. As in nature, the characteristics of vata include movement, lightness, and dryness. This dosha controls the biological movement in our body, such as our breathing, our heartbeat, the movement of food through our body, the movement that leads to excretion. Vata also controls certain functions in the mind and central nervous system that relate to movement and direction. Vata animates us and initiates the important processes that keep the body alive.

PITTA

The second dosha is *pitta*, which represents the element of fire combined with a minimum of the element of water. Pitta, representing transformation, is behind the creation of bodily tissue, and controls digestive fires that transform food so that it can be absorbed into the body. Pitta converts the water and air that enters the body. It controls all secretions, including enzymes and hormones, the body's energy, and the body's temperature. In nature, pitta is associated with the properties of the sun and fire—heat and penetration. Pitta also manifests the characteristic of Agni and enlightenment. Pitta helps us to absorb knowledge and understand it.

KAPHA

The third dosha is *kapha* and represents a combination of the element of water and the element of earth. In nature, this dosha is equated with the moon and water, and shares the characteristics of liquidity, heaviness or density, quiescence, and coldness. Kapha represents preservation. It maintains the body's strength, lubricates the body's joints and tissues, and provides moisture to the skin. It helps bind us together and protect our immunity. Kapha also helps us preserve or retain the knowledge that we acquire.

AYURVEDA RECOGNIZES THAT we are born with a certain combination of these three doshas; and that this combination is what distinguishes us from one another. In Vedic terms, our personal combination of the tridoshas is defined by our prakriti (our nature: body type, emotional make-up, and the quality of our mind). An ayurvedic diagnosis would identify our particular configuration of the tridoshas, then use the original balance as a marker to help us maintain good health.

By paying strict attention to the tridoshas, ayurveda can determine if our body is sliding out of balance. By observing the direction of the imbalance, ayurveda can also determine if our body is developing a predisposition toward a particular illness before we exhibit or even feel its symptoms. This gives us a head start at attacking the illness. But to solve the imbalance, the ayurveda remedy is reversal—the restoration of the original balance of the elements, which is the same approach followed by vastu.

All the ayurveda methods used to correct the imbalance and repair the body's natural defense mechanisms are holistic: the correction of one's diet, the promotion of a healthy lifestyle, and a healthy environment to create harmony and peace. If a patient is already suffering from a specific illness, an ayurveda doctor (ved) will also use cures or tonics. Every one of these remedies are natural; they are never synthetic.

Vastu also plays a role in the tridoshas. It can help maintain the balance in your particular dosha or combination of doshas by simply adhering to an important ayurveda rule: like increases like. For example, say an individual has a vata constitution. Vata is connected to air, so in the practice of vastu, one would be careful not to sleep in the northwest quadrant of the home. Someone with a vata constitution would also try not to work in the northwest quadrant of a space, whether you work at home or at a company. These two activities—sleeping and working—consume most of our time. Because like increases like, spending so many hours in the northwest quadrant of air could create an imbalance in the vata constitution and trigger illnesses and afflictions associated with this dosha, such as chronic coughs and fatigue.

If one has a pitta dosha, which is associated with fire, or a kapha dosha, which is associated with water, one would follow the same rule: like increases like. Someone with a pitta dosha would try not to sleep or work in the southeast quadrant, which belongs to the realm of fire. Someone with a kapha dosha would try not to sleep or work in the northeast quadrant, which is the realm of water. By spending too much time in the quadrant associated with our particular constitution, we run the risk of creating an imbalance since like increases like. And an imbalance jeopardizes our well-being.

Because ayurveda is also related to Soma, the god of health, who reigns in the north, the north part of any vastu space is associated with good healing properties. We should try to store our medicines in the north to reap these benefits.

TRIGUNAS

As an adjunct to the tridoshas, ayurveda developed the theory of the *trigunas*, which represent the three characteristics that exist in the mind in a specific proportion that is determined at creation. This theory is also important to yoga.

1. *Sattva*, the highest guna, creates a mind with illumination, intelligence, purity, stability. People dominated by sattva tend to be intelligent, pure, creative, and spiritual, and reveal a wealth of kindness and compassion.
2. *Rajas*, the middle guna, fills the mind with action, motion, restlessness. People dominated by rajas tend to be ambitious, hyperactive, hardworking, prosperous, extroverted. They can have strong egos and be quick to change their mind.
3. *Tamas*, the lowest guna, overwhelms the mind with illusion, static resistance and dullness and causes negative and harmful actions.

86

People dominated by tamas tend to be lazy, ignorant, lack personal hygiene, and can be selfish.

Ayurveda works to keep a proper ratio among the trigunas by advocating healthy thoughts and actions that improve the level of sattva and by discouraging negative thoughts and actions that create too much ragas and tamas. The mind is healthier and less likely to precipitate an illness in the body if the trigunas favor the qualities of sattva. For this reason, ayurveda also recommends the practice of yoga, especially asanas, or poses. By altering and improving our state of mind, yoga can reduce the proportion of rajas and tamas in relation to sattva.

Vastu can also give a boost to sattva. In our practice of vastu, we want to pay particular attention to the northeast quadrant. Overseen by the deity Isa and the element of water, the northeast is the gateway to the gods and gives us positive cosmic energy. In order to receive the benefits of this quadrant—serenity, peace, purity—all of which are important characteristics connected to the sattvic mind, try not to block the energy of the northeast quadrant with heavy or tall objects. If there are walls in your home or office that close off the northeast corner, don't worry. You don't need to tear down the walls to unblock the northeast. In the course of the book, you will learn how to make a symbolic correction that can resolve the problem.

THE IMPORTANCE OF RHYTHM
AND PROPER PROPORTIONS

The three Vedic sciences, vastu, ayurveda, and yoga, all recognize the importance of rhythm and proper proportions, two principles that reflect the laws of nature and dualities. In ayurveda and yoga, rhythm and proportion are exhibited in many ways. Both sciences recognize that the state of our mind influences the health of our body. When we suffer from depression, emotional turmoil of any kind, including too much stress or tension, our body pays a price. We get run down, exhausted, sick. In vastu, rhythm

87

reflects the cycles of the universe and creates a physical space that allows us to honor these cycles and live in harmony with them, not discord.

AYURVEDA AND DIET

Principles of proper rhythm and proportion can be seen in the ayurveda diet. In New Delhi, I met Anurag Sharma, the chief executive of Shree Baidyanath Ayurved Bhawan Limited, India's oldest manufacturer of ayurveda products. "Most of our health problems are related to what we eat, how we eat, and what time we eat," Anurag told me. He stated that we must always eat according to the balance of our particular doshas and emphasized the importance of paying attention to the cycle of time and seasons, and the daily weather.

The body prefers seasonal food based on its own climate, not the climate in the opposite hemisphere. Paying attention to the seasons also means that we would eat more cold foods in the summer and warmer foods in the winter. This theory is based on the law of nature. In the warm weather, the excessive heat aggravates our body, so cold food cools us down. The reverse is true in the winter. Of course this can be difficult to do depending on where one lives, not to mention that we've become so accustomed to eating foods out of season. But to the extent that one can eat seasonally, the body will tend to respond with good health.

The importance of proportion and rhythm runs through all the rules that govern our diet. We must be careful not to disturb our digestive cycle, which means that we must eat at proper intervals. And if we eat too much food or food that is too heavy, we can irritate our stomach. In ayurveda, proportion and rhythm are as important as maintaining a diet specific to our particular dosha or combination of doshas.

BREATH AND VIBRATION

Yoga also stresses the importance of rhythm and proportion. Creative energy or cosmic breath, the vibration that led to the primordial word, AUM, set everything in motion and initiated creation—the presence of all that exists and all that will come into existence. This creative energy is also called *prana* (energy or life force). Prana energizes our physical and mental activities, serving as a link between the body and mind.

Yoga teaches us the importance of our prana through the practice of asanas and pranayama, which lead to the rhythmic control of our inhalation and exhalation of the breath. Through proper inhalation and exhalation, we take full advantage of the cosmic energy and prana, which leads to spiritual, physical, and mental well-being. B. K. S. Iyengar offers this explanation:

> When you inhale, the self comes into contact with the body. Hence, inhalation is the evolution of the soul towards the body and the spiritual cosmic breath coming into contact with the individual breath. Exhalation, from the point of view of physical health, is removal of toxins from the system. From the psychological point of view, it quiets the mind. From the spiritual point of view, it is the individual breath in the person coming into contact with external cosmic breath so that they are one.[21]

Asanas and pranayama slowly subjugate the ego, mind, and intelligence. This allows us to turn inward and stay focused on the spiritual part of ourselves, which leads us slowly forward on the path of the goal in yoga. The yogi, who has gone through a lifetime of unwavering dedication to develop perfect attention and attentiveness, finds that sublime moment when the body's vibration pulsates to the rhythm of the cosmic energy. This is what vastu brings into the construction of the Kandariya Mahadeva. The rhythms of the vibrations in the sacred womb chamber reflect the rhythm of the

---

[21] B. K. S. Iyengar, *The Tree of Yoga*, ed. Daniel Rivers-Moore, (New Delhi: HarperCollins Publishers India, 1998).

89

vibrations of the cosmic energy that set creation in motion. They have the power of AUM.

Through the practice of asanas and the proper rhythm of inhalation and exhalation, we become attuned to our own vibrations. We learn how to discipline them through our breathing. We learn to reinforce positive vibrations that enhance our spiritual growth and overall well-being. We learn to shut out negative vibrations, which make us angry, depressed, tense—any emotion that interferes with our inner peace. This is why ayurveda encourages the practice of yoga's asanas and pranayama. They give us control over the mind and bring us in touch with the soul so that we can stay healthy.

Vastu, as we know, pays attention to the vibrations in our environment. In the ideal home and workspace, the energy vibrates at the same frequency that our body and environment do. Vastu does to the home what yoga does to the body and mind. It helps the positive energy to *circulate* around us and within us. Of course, there will be negative energies, too, but they must flow. They must be in movement and not become stagnant or trapped.

All three disciplines are about harmony, balance, rhythm, and proportion. Through ayurveda, one can maintain the appropriate balance within the body and stay healthy. Through yoga, we discover a sense of quietude for body, mind, and soul. Through vastu, one's house becomes a temple, a healthy home for the soul.

Before I left India and returned to New York, I saw my friend Sudesh one last time. We sat, had tea, laughed, discussed much of what I had learned. Then, Sudesh gave me a poem that he had written.

ODE TO THE UNIVERSE

❦

At the edge of the universe,
I sit on the last precipice, contemplating
The Great Wind blows,
The Fabric of the universe flutters above,
Legs dangle,
The abysmal abyss below
On the dark canvas, stretched by timeless span,
The eternal silence holding my hand,
I watch the dance of sparks,
Galaxies hugging, swirling, moving on and on
Rocks fly hither thither, and then
The Explosion of Countless suns,
The Sound of the Great Word echoes forever
And then it dissolves,
Oh, universe! You are THAT.

PART TWO

CREATING A HOME
FOR THE SOUL

A human being is a part of a whole, called by us "universe," a part limited in time and space. He experiences himself, his thoughts and feelings as something separated from the rest . . . a kind of optical delusion of his consciousness. This delusion is a kind of prison for us, restricting us to our personal desires and to affection for a few persons nearest to you. Our task must be to free ourselves from this prison by widening our circle of compassion to embrace all living creatures and the whole of nature in its beauty.

—ALBERT EINSTEIN

Now that we have explored vastu's roots and basic principles, it is time to turn our attention to how you can work with vastu in your home and workspace. As you begin to put vastu into practice in Part Two, it is important to remember that the science is flexible. Vastu living does not lay out hard and fast rules. There is not just one single way to set up a space in your home or workplace. If you can arrange your home or workspace so that just 50 percent is per vastu living, you're doing great.

Remember that your house or apartment or condominium or cooperative is a living organism. This is equally true with your workspace. Vastu living's objective is to help you align the vibrations of this living organism with your own body's vibrations. You want to establish a harmonious environment that increases your positive vibrations. No matter what, you don't want to encourage disharmony or discord. This harmony is achieved by adhering to the law of nature, by accepting that everything is divine and worthy of our respect, and by providing a harmonious relationship between 1) your self, your home, and your workplace and 2) the five elements of space, air, fire, water, and earth.

It is also important to recognize and accept that individuals in a home or individuals at work have distinct personalities and specific needs that require thoughtful choices. Again, vastu living does provide choice, and making wise choices helps create that harmonious relationship between you (and anyone who lives with or shares space with you), your physical spaces, and your surrounding exterior environment. Proper choices mean that you (and your soul) will have a nurturing home. I find this analogy to be useful: The soul should be thought of as a deity, and your personal space, whether a home or workplace, should be thought of as a temple. If we treat our spaces as sacred spaces, we find that connection between our soul and the Supreme Creator. We see that we are That. We find inner peace.

Chapter 5 gets you started in your practice of vastu with a questionnaire, based on the tridosha system in ayurveda, that helps you know yourself and your pattern of preferences and dislikes. This chapter also shows you how to create your vastu blueprints. The next three chapters (6 through 8) guide you in the practice of vastu at home and at work, and the use of nature on the property and inside the home. Chapter 9 provides symbolic remedies that can counteract imbalances that may exist in your space and interfere with your goal for harmony and inner peace.

You certainly don't need to be a Hindu to reap the benefits of vastu living, any more than you need to be Hindu to do yoga, practice meditation, or follow ayurveda. Vastu living can work anywhere, and for people who practice any faith. It can even work for those of us who are spiritually inclined but do not follow a specific religion. Vastu living only asks you to consider your interconnectedness with the Divine—the divinity in all life forms, the divinity of the earth on which you live, and the divinity of the entire cosmos.

So, get out your compass and pencil and start mapping your new vastu home or office. And please plan to tinker and fine tune your home and workplace over a period of time. Even after you have created your vastu living layouts, you will probably shift around some furniture until it looks right and *feels* right to your innermost self.

And while you're doing all this tinkering, you will also be learning to be aware of your interconnectedness with everything that exists around you. You will be discovering—and hopefully discarding—anything that has been creating disharmony, and becoming aware of the deep significance of your design and décor decisions. You will learn how these decisions can block or promote the inner peace that can be yours through vastu living.

Once this process is finished, think of how wonderful it will be to enter your home and pause to soak up the good feelings that come from your vastu living space. Imagine the joy you'll feel to have that same positive experience at work. This is what vastu living is all about: the creation of a sacred and welcoming space for your soul.

VASTU LIVING:
WHAT YOU NEED

You need the following to create vastu living in your property, in your home and in your work-space:

- completed questionnaire (see Chapter 5, *Getting Started*);

- numerous copies of the diagram of the vastu purusha mandala (see pp. 241–245 for mandala and rectangular orientations to clip-and-copy for the creation of your own blueprints);

- your personal vastu living kit:

  —a pocket-size compass that includes the intermediate directions (NE, SE, SW, and NW) and the cardinal directions (N, E, S, W);
  —metal measuring tape;
  —various appeasement aids (see Chapter 9, *Appeasing the Gods— Appeasing Your Soul*)

❀ 5 ❀

GETTING STARTED

A careful observation will show that the heaven is there on earth,
not in the sky above.

—MAHATMA GANDHI

DETERMINING YOUR NEEDS AND PREFERENCES

THE PHYSICAL SPACES where we spend most of our time have a pivotal effect on us, and vastu is here to help us ensure that the effect is positive. A first crucial step is to be sure we know our selves so that our home and workspace can truly reflect our personalities and be aligned to our personal needs. To this end, I am including a short questionnaire on ayurveda, the Vedic science of life, to help you determine your dosha (body type, emotional make-up, and quality of mind). The doshas, as you'll recall from Chapter 4, are a kind of classification system having to do

with our basic constitution. By knowing which dosha is dominant in *you*, you can see how it bears on your pattern of preferences and dislikes, and your level of comfort or discomfort in your home and workspace. Once you can see your natural biases clearly and plainly, you will be able to make the appropriate choices and calculations so that vastu living will work best for you.

Please use a separate piece of paper to fill in your answers. This questionnaire is about *you*, so there are no "right" or "wrong" answers. Just take your time and try to be as objective as possible. You want to see more than what is reflected back at you from the mirror. As with so much of vastu, impulsive answers or decisions can interfere with success.

If you live with a roommate or partner, ask him or her to fill out the questionnaire. It is useful to see how your needs coincide or differ. It also helps to have a good friend or relative—someone who sees you frequently—complete a questionnaire. Their answers will reflect their impression of you and can be very instructive.

VASTU LIVING QUESTIONNAIRE
FOR DETERMINING YOUR NEEDS AND PREFERENCES

1. What bothers you more: (a) weather that is cold and dry, (b) hot and sunny, or (c) cold and damp?
2. When things don't go your way, do you tend to get (a) fearful and anxious, (b) angry and upset, or (c) tolerant and forgiving?
3. Do you have (a) limited stamina, (b) moderate stamina or (c) tremendous stamina?
4. Do you sleep (a) lightly for about five hours and toss and turn? Do you get by with (b) five to seven hours of sleep? Do you need (c) at least eight hours of sleep?
5. Are you (a) chronically thin, (b) the right weight for your size, or (c) chronically overweight?
6. Do you (a) find it difficult to gain weight, or do you gain weight (b)

in appropriate relation to your activities and diet, or (c) at the mere smell of food?

7. Do you (a) change your mind easily, (b) make quick and firm decisions, or (c) take your time to say yes or no?

8. Is your memory (a) poor, (b) reasonably good, or (c) excellent?

9. Are you (a) very active, (b) moderately active, or (c) lazy—happiest when you are watching someone else work out?

10. When you are active, do you (a) move around quickly, (b) move at a moderate speed, or (c) move at a snail's pace?

11. Do you (a) occasionally skip meals and then eat a lot or a little food—whatever suits you at that moment? Are you (b) always ready to eat a big meal or do you (c) prefer to eat smaller meals?

12. Do you (a) talk fast and frequently interrupt someone else who is speaking? Do you (b) speak with persuasion so that you usually win arguments, or do you (c) speak in a low voice with a soft and measured tone?

13. Do you have (a) limited physical strength, (b) moderate physical strength, (c) great physical strength?

14. Is your level of thirst (a) constantly changing, (b) excessive, or (c) very low?

15. Is your mood (a) unpredictable, (b) often intense, or (c) calm and steady?

EVALUATING THE ANSWERS

Once you have gathered the completed questionnaires, read through them carefully and compare the answers. Remember that the answers given by a friend or relative can provide details about you that can be very useful as you begin to create a vastu living home or workspace.

If you chose *a* for the majority of the answers, then your constitution shows the likelihood of a vata (air) dosha. If you chose *b*, then your constitution shows the likelihood of a pitta (fire) dosha. If you chose *c*, your constitution shows a likely kapha (water) dosha.

You may even discover that your answers divide fairly evenly between two of the doshas. The important point here is that these responses give you an indication of your constitution, a factor you will want to consider, especially when you choose where to sleep and work—the two activities that involve most of your time. Please remember the ayurveda rule: like increases like. If you spend too much time in a quadrant overseen by the element that is also dominant in your body, you can trigger an unhealthy imbalance in your body. If, for example, you have a vata (air) constitution and you find your memory not just poor but declining, you could be spending too much time in the northwest realm, which belongs to the element of air. Are you sleeping and working in this quadrant? If so, like increases like and leads to excess vata in your body, which could interfere with your well-being (refer back to Chapter 4, *Vastu and the Vedic View of Health,* if necessary.)

So expect to play around a bit with the elements that relate specifically to your dosha or combination of doshas. The bottom line with vastu is that the choices should *feel* right. Analyze the effect of the various elements on your body—see what makes you feel good, see what increases your feeling of harmony and inner peace. Everything should be balanced; you don't want to have too much of the element or elements that dominate your dosha constitution.

Do you live with someone who has a different constitution? Do you share the same bedroom? Then try to place the bedroom in a quadrant that is safe—a quadrant that does not violate the rule of like increases like for either of you. A safe location for both of you would be a bedroom in the southwest of the home. If that location is not possible, then try to place the bed in the southwest quadrant within your existing bedroom. Do you share a workspace with someone who has a different constitution? Again, if the workspace is located in a quadrant that is unhealthy for either one of you, try to shift it to a safe quadrant. Or at least try to shift the placement of each desk within the present space, so that both of you are sitting in the realm of an element that is not the same as the element that dominates your constitution.

Reassessing, thinking carefully, testing choices to keep the elements in harmony by aligning them with your self and with your home and your workspace—this is the right way to move forward with vastu. This is how you create a home for the soul. And this is the ultimate goal in vastu living.

EXPRESSING YOUR SELF

Your ability to express your personality in your home and workspace is another important factor that adds to the harmony that exists between you and your space. And you aren't the only one who feels this harmony. Everyone who enters the space feels good sitting there. This harmony is especially important in your workspace, where you spend so much of your time. If your personal environment does not serve as an extension of your personality, then that space will not work for you.

When you walk into someone's home, doesn't your eye tend to go to the paintings or photographs or displays of objects from trips or collections that appear to have a repetitive theme? These visual displays connect us to the person who lives there. At times, we may even feel a bit of a snoop as we admire these bits and pieces of an identity or identities. But these clues in a décor make the space a home, not a makeshift set.

When you do have a favorite space in your home or workspace, very often this space feels uniquely your own. If you take a good look around a favorite area, doesn't the décor reflect your interests, your joys, your tastes, ultimately your self? It usually does.

So look carefully at your present home and workspace. Does each space identify itself and speak to you? Does it reflect your personality and preferences? Or do certain areas make you feel aloof and uncomfortable? At work, for example, do you feel that your workspace gives an accurate impression of who you are, or could another person take it over without anyone noticing the change? If that's the case, something's amiss.

Of course, if you share a home or workspace with other people, their identities should also be reflected. The point is, when we enter a room, an office, a home, we should feel that we know something about the people who live there.

CREATING YOUR SPIRITUAL BLUEPRINTS

PLEASE NOTE: If you live in the southern hemisphere, you will need to shift everything on the vastu purusha mandala 90 degrees to the right. For example, any advice that suggests the northeast would mean the southeast in the southern hemisphere.

To create your vastu blueprints, you need a compass, preferably one that includes the intermediate directions (NE, SE, SW, NW), sheets of paper, and a pencil. You will also need the vastu purusha mandala pullout, which you'll find on p. 000. This mandala, with its valuable vastu guidelines, is your reference and in some cases your actual blueprint. Don't worry. You don't need to be an artist or architect to make your layouts. We're talking about rough drawings here.

PERFECTION IN A SQUARE

As explained in Chapter 2, *The Vastu Purusha Mandala*, the vastu spiritual blueprint, takes the shape of the square, which Hindus consider the most perfect form. The square stands as a symbol of the Vedic view of the universe. In theory, this shape of the mandala is the model to use for the layout of a physical space or site so that it, too, reflects the universe and its perfect expression of harmony and balance. In your practice of vastu, however, some of your physical spaces or your site may not be in the shape of a square. But when they are square-shaped or nearly square-shaped, use enlarged copies of the vastu purusha mandala pullout to create the layout.

RECTANGULAR SPACES

If you have a rectangular-shaped property or physical space, you can still use the vastu purusha mandala as a reference. The rectangles shown below are reproduced in the back of the book so you can clip and copy. Choose the one that most closely matches the orientation of the rectangle on your site or physical space. The four boxes demarcated by the lines that intersect in the center define the important quadrants.

FIGURES 27

Diagram of Quadrants for a Rectangle East and West

FIGURES 28

Diagram of Quadrants for a Rectangle North and South

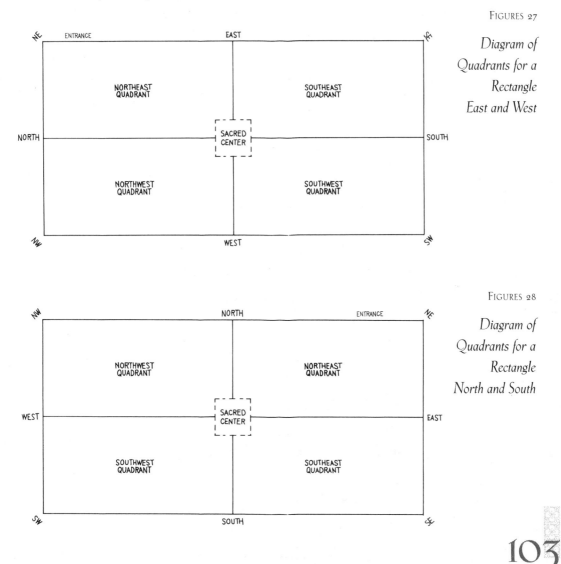

103

L-Shaped Spaces

If you have an L-shaped property, home, workspace, or room, simply divide the property into a rectangle and square or two rectangles. Then use the vastu purusha mandala for a square space, located at the back of the book, and a copy of the properly oriented rectangle for the rectangular shape, also found at the back. Each shape should incorporate one side of the L. (See Figure 32, below.) Then, even though they are physically connected, treat each mandala as a separate mandala. Properly align the orientation of the quadrants of each mandala with the physical space or property. Follow this same procedure to determine the layout of a split-level home or business.

FIGURE 29

Diagram of an L–Shaped Home or Property

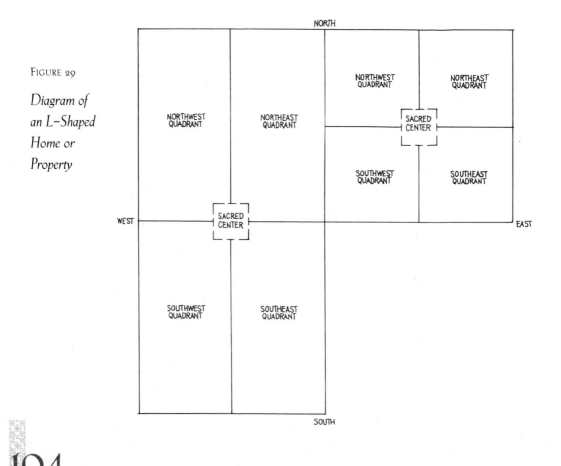

Quirky Spaces

Very often a property, a building, even a room can have an area that juts out at an odd angle, or the entire shape of the space doesn't conform to a true square or a rectangle. Your property may have a quirky shape, with acres of natural woods or pastureland or a strange circle or triangle at one end. In this situation, just mark off the area on the property that you actually use —the landscaped area—into a square or rectangle, and base your blueprint on that part of the site. With a building or an interior space that is a quirky shape, just choose the blueprint of a square or rectangle, whichever is closest to the overall shape.

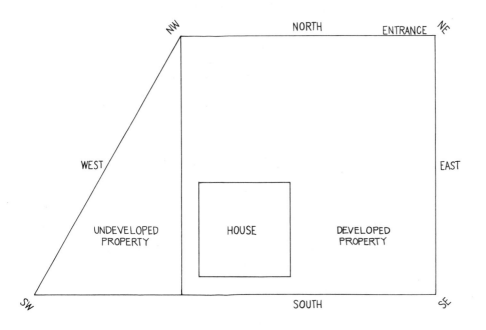

FIGURE 30

Diagram of the "Quirky" Site

DETERMINING YOUR
NUMBER OF BLUEPRINTS

Make enlarged copies of the vastu purusha mandala pull-out and the rectangular blueprints before you actually start to fill in the layouts; it will be easier to make your notations and drawings on a larger surface. You will want to make enough blueprints to cover any of the following environments that relate to your personal space:

- the property surrounding your workspace or house that you have landscaped for use, including activities, such as tennis and swimming;

- the interior of your home or workspace—one for each floor if you have multiple floors, and each room in your home or workspace, including patios, terraces, balconies, and sitting porches—every space that you use.

If you live or work in a loft or a wall-less space, then make a copy for each designated area. In the home, this might include bedroom area(s), kitchen area, workspace, living room, dining room, bathroom.

EXTERIOR BLUEPRINTS

If you have exterior grounds, walk slowly around the property and, using the compass, determine the orientation of any slopes and elevations. If there is a slope, note the direction of the decline on your vastu purusha blueprint. If there is an elevation, note its location. Mark down the location of the fencing, trees, shrubbery, gardens, swimming pool, and ponds. Indicate the location of trees that are taller than your home or workspace. Mark down the placement of the driveway or walkway that leads into your property and the location of the entrance door to your home or business.

Note all of this information on the exterior blueprint and place everything in its proper location: the northwest, north, northeast, east, southeast, south, southwest, west, or the center. Again, your drawing can be simple, but try to get the ratio correct. For example, if you have an ornamental pool in the northeast, draw a small circle that approximates its size in relation to the size of the blueprint. If you have a tall oak in the southwest, you could just mark an *x* and indicate tall tree or oak.

INTERIOR BLUEPRINTS

Your next blueprint should determine the orientation and location of the spaces in the interior of your home or business. Note the locations of all the doors, including the exit and entrance doors and entrances into each room. You do not need to worry about closet doors. Be sure to include every room or space, from the bathroom to a terrace. The objective is to determine the relationship between the elements and their placement within your personal space.

BLUEPRINTS FOR EACH ROOM

One of the easiest ways to make a room layout is to stand in the center of a room and just rotate slowly around. Note on the blueprint the cardinal or midpoint location of all the built-in structures, such as bookcases and cabinets and closets. Also include the windows, big appliances, and all the furniture and the doors in and out of the room. If you have plants in a room, don't forget to include them on the blueprint. If you have electrical systems, such as a stereo, computer, or television, please indicate them as well.

If you live or work in a loft or wall-less space, you still need to treat each space as you would a room, so just imagine that there are walls that separate the areas of the loft. Each area will still have a north, south, east, and west, and the intermediate directions with their corresponding elements and deities, including the element of space and Brahma in the sacred center. Then proceed as above.

EVALUATING YOUR BLUEPRINTS—GENERAL GUIDELINES

Aligning the Elements

When you examine your blueprints, see how well the existing layouts conform to the location of the five elements and their deities as they appear on the chart below. The center of each blueprint is the Brahmasthana, the sacred realm of Brahma and the element of space. This is also the location of most of the important vulnerable points on the vastu purusha. So this particular part of each space should be treated with care and not overburdened by weight. Don't panic if your home or business is plunk on the middle of the Brahmasthana; we will deal with that in due course, and not through demolition! You may not be able to protect the center of a building either, but you may be able to protect the Brahmasthana of each room.

Intermediate Directions

Direction	Element	Deity
Northeast	Water	Isa
Southeast	Fire	Agni
Southwest	Earth	Pitri
Northwest	Air	Vayu
Center	Space	Brahma

CONSIDER YOUR PERSONAL NEEDS

Keep in mind your personal needs and preferences, which were determined in the above questionnaire. If your particular constitution—vata (air), pitta (fire), or kapha (water)—reveals an unhealthy balance, let your home and workspace contribute to your cure.

Renovations and Alterations? Proceed with Care

If you are planning a renovation, remember: buildings and their surrounding environment are organisms that emit their own vibrations. Modifications to the structure of any space can disturb the harmony of the vibrations, which can in turn harm you. So be careful with renovations, alterations, and remodeling.

First draw a design of your intended changes on a copy of your vastu blueprint. See if your plans disturb the elements assigned to each quadrant. If you notice that your changes could cause a problem, play it safe and appease any element and its deity that may be disturbed. The disturbance could have a negative impact on you.

For example, you may be planning to expand your kitchen. When you create your blueprint, you notice that your new sink, which obviously uses water, is going to be placed in the quadrant of the kitchen that belongs to the element of fire. If you can't shift the sink, then this is a situation in which you would make an appeasement: The element of water will be trespassing into the realm of the element of fire and this can cause problems. You will want to placate both of these elements: water because it has been displaced from its correct quadrant, and fire because its realm has been violated by the presence of water. (See Chapter 9, *Appease the Gods—Appease Your Soul.*)

Some renovations, however, can be highly beneficial. For instance, lots of walls in a space can impede the free flow of vibrations, the positive cosmic energy, and the positive flow of spiritual power. Removing walls and creating some wall-less environments allow these flowing energies and vibrations to move around more freely through the space. Adding built-in bookcases

109

and cabinets in the southern end of any room, especially in the southwestern quadrant, will retain these positive energies.

Planning a Move

Moving into a new house or office space? Just the thought of a move makes most of us weary. The long job of unpacking and arranging furniture tires us out and we usually end up leaving some of the furniture and many of our personal belongings where they drop. As long as we don't trip over them and as long as their location doesn't aesthetically offend us, we leave the chair, statue, and television alone and don't think about their effect on our personal harmony.

There is, of course, a better way to proceed. *Before you move*, create a set of vastu blueprints of your new home or new business office and each of its interior rooms or spaces. On each room blueprint, you can place your possessions where they belong according to vastu living. Not only is this an efficient way to get settled into your new space, it will cut down the number of times you have to lift and lug in the future. No need to create disharmony by putting objects and furniture in the wrong places.

You may still end up shifting around a few objects and pieces of furniture. What you thought was right may not work once you move into the new space. Each structure has its own vibrations. So, again, just accept that the successful creation of a vastu space is a *process* that takes time. But by first planning out your move on a set of blueprints, you will be ahead of the game.

Now it's time to use your spiritual blueprints in your practice of vastu living. We will start by optimizing the level of harmony in your home, then move on to your workspace.

✾ 6 ✾

VASTU LIVING AT HOME

To destroy anything is easy. To build requires great skill and care.

—MAHATMA GANDHI

THE VASTU HOME

A vastu living home should bring us pleasure when our eyes gaze over each space, including the kitchen and bathroom. And this pleasure should be deep and internal, creating a sense of well-being whenever we are inside the home or walking around the property if we live in a home that has land.

How do we achieve this level of pleasure? When we start the process of turning a house or apartment or loft into a vastu living home, we make the entire space cohesive, and express the concept of interconnectedness.

Whether we live in a studio apartment in the city or in a house in the country with lots of property, each area within a space and the collection of spaces should feel interlinked and part of the whole. This connection should also extend to the land that immediately surrounds the home. We establish this connection by 1) honoring the five elements, and 2) honoring our personality and the personalities of the occupants, and establishing their identities in our space.

HARMONY IN THEMES AND PATTERNS

From a small apartment room to a home with multiple floors, it is important to establish themes or subtle patterns that move through the space. Choose two or three of your favorite colors and let them flow through the décor of the home. Use them in different ways—sometimes as a dominant color painted on the walls of a room or incorporated into the wallpaper; sometimes as a secondary color in cushions, in a rug, in the table linen, or in the window treatment. You may, of course, use more than three colors in your home. The idea is to have your favorite two or three colors reappear in different ways throughout the interior. This recurrence creates an appealing rhythm and unites the many spaces or rooms into one cohesive whole that is identified with you.

You might take family heirlooms or a favorite collection and display treasured items in your various rooms. This relatedness again creates cohesion and harmony. The conscientious and deliberate continuation binds you personally to the home and makes you feel that the home is part of you.

Over time, as your personality gets incorporated into your home, you will feel this harmony and rhythm wash over you and slowly remove your tension. If this all seems too great a leap in faith, consider this. We breathe rhythmically, and when that rhythm is disrupted, we notice it—fast. Automatically, our body works to reestablish the former rhythm. We benefit from the rhythm of our breath, which is something we also learn in yoga.

NATURE—THE KEY TO RHYTHM

Vastu recognizes that our dwellings should reflect the rhythm of the universe and our connection to all of nature. And there are so many ways to do this. You can bring plants and natural products, such as clay pots, jute baskets, sisal rugs, or dried flowers, into your home. This is an easy way to create harmony between the interior of your home and the world outside your home, especially if you live in an asphalt jungle. When nature feels remote, we must give it a presence in our home.

Nature brings its own rhythm to the home. A plant, for instance, has its cycle of life. The sun also has its universal rhythm that connects to all life forms and sustains us. We all react to the rhythm inherent in the sun's daily movement and to its more subtle annual changes, which affect our climate and seasons. We look forward to the gentle morning sun, if it flows into our home, and to the benefit that comes from the earliest rays.

The sun is symbolic of spiritual light and enlightenment. When Hindus face the east to pray or meditate, they are paying homage to the sun. In vastu living, if we face east when we study or read, we are more likely to absorb knowledge. Many Hindus who practice vastu, especially students and scholars, even prefer to sleep with their head in the east, so that they can soak in enlightenment and inspiration during the nighttime. Many Hindus face east when they bathe in the morning. Their bath is considered an act of cleansing that includes spiritual purification.

Nighttime activities occur in the west, the realm of the setting sun and the point where the journey leads into darkness and finally back to the quiet reawakening of the sun. Your own body follows this same rhythm. The majority of us prefer to work in the day and sleep at night. When your home acknowledges the natural harmony that defines the universe, your home also reinforces the natural harmony that exists within your self.

MAKE ROOM FOR PEACE AND SERENITY

An essential part of any vastu living home is a zone of tranquility. In a Hindu home, this zone would be a puja (prayer) room. Our zone of tranquility is a place where we can quiet down and our body can relax, where we try to forget our stress and anxiety and negativity. This is a space where human-made problems are left behind like a wet umbrella at the door. The zone of tranquility, which should not be confused with the Brahmasthana or sacred center of a room, can be its own room or a part of a room. If you have the space to devote a whole room to the tranquility zone, you might want to create a personal shrine for it, some focal point to honor a deity or someone who for you symbolizes compassion, love, and inner calm. Your zone of tranquility should be a place where you can shut the door and meditate, do yoga, or just concentrate on rhythmic breathing.

FIGURE 31

*Small
Zone of
Tranquility*

If you do not have the space to allocate an entire room or a fair-sized area in a wall-less space to a zone of tranquility, you can set up a zone within a quadrant or set up a couple of quiet places in other rooms. A zone of tranquility can celebrate an aspect of nature or a source of inspiration that becomes the focus for your eyes at the start of meditation. It can be a rocking chair placed near a window with a view of the sunrise or a graceful tree by a pond. It can be an easy chair by a side table with a small collection of seashells found on the shore or special stones carried back from a hike or trek. If your home is limited to one small room, you can just take a mat or a towel and unroll it to create a temporary designated zone of tranquility, near a special photo or special hanging on the wall.

Music can also be a great addition to your zone of tranquility. You might turn on classical music, meditation music—any form of music that carries you away from your concerns and empties your mind. What you're looking for is a source of positive vibration that soothes the vibrations in your body.

You can also consider a special place outdoors for your own zone of tranquility. Listen to the sounds of nature. The chattering of birds, the dramatic buzz of cicadas, the rustling of leaves—these sounds tend to calm the inner self.

HONOR THE DIVINE ESSENCE

You'll recall that earlier we compared vastu living to the creation of a temple for the soul, that divine part of us that is connected to the essence of the Supreme Creator. In vastu living, we think of our homes as sacred temples, too—temples for body, mind, and spirit. In India, for instance, many Hindus adhere to the tradition of removing their shoes just before they enter a home or immediately after they cross the threshold. When they take off their shoes, they are repeating an act that they faithfully follow whenever they visit a temple. The filth of the streets and the world's impurities are kept outside; the interior of the home is kept sacred.

NOBLE FOOTSTEPS

❦

If you remove your shoes once you enter your home, you are respecting an old tradition that was followed by Mahatma Gandhi. Slip on a pair of wood sandals. They are good for the feet. They are also wonderful "climatic controls." In winter, they keep your feet warm. In summer, they keep your feet cool.

FIGURE 32

Mahatma Gandhi

YOUR HOME IS YOUR TEMPLE

There are many symbolic connections between a traditional Hindu home and the Hindu temple. Many older Indian homes have an interior center courtyard, called the Brahmasthana. The most sacred part of the house, the Brahmasthana is similar to the inner sanctum of the temple where spiritual power radiates in every direction. If you happen to have a home with an open courtyard in the center, treat it as the most holy part of the home, the spiritual center, and let its power flow through you. If you don't have a central courtyard, then try to keep the center of each room free of furniture so that the spiritual power can collect there and radiate in all directions. Connecting with this spiritual power will help to reinforce your consciousness of your own divine essence.

ORIENTATION AND SHAPE

PLEASE NOTE: If you live in the southern hemisphere, you will need to shift everything on the vastu purusha mandala 90 degrees to the right. For example, any advice that suggests the northeast would mean the southeast in the southern hemisphere; the south would mean west; etc.

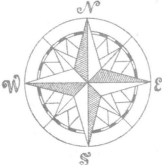

If you live in an apartment building or loft, then your focus will be on your interior space and its relationship to the cardinal and intermediate directions and their corresponding elements. If you live in a home with property, you will want to be sure that the land, which also contains the five elements, is in harmony with the home and with your inner self.

CARDINAL DIRECTIONS

NORTH

DEITY:
Soma and Kuber

IDENTIFICATION:
Health and Wealth

WEST

DEITY:
Varuma

IDENTIFICATION:
Unknown and Darkness

EAST

DEITY:
Surya

IDENTIFICATION:
Enlightenment and Inspiration

SOUTH

DEITY:
Yama

IDENTIFICATION:
Death, Duty, and Responsibility

INTERMEDIATE DIRECTIONS

NORTHWEST

ELEMENT:
Air

DEITY:
Vayu

NORTHEAST

ELEMENT:
Water

DEITY:
Isa

CENTER

ELEMENT:
Space

DEITY:
Brahma

SOUTHWEST

ELEMENT:
Earth

DEITY:
Pitri

SOUTHEAST

ELEMENT:
Fire

DEITY:
Agni

ORIENTATION OF THE SITE AND HOME

If the entrance to your property is in the north or the east of the north-east corner, this creates an open space in the northeast quadrant, which we call the gateway to the gods. An east-facing house receives the benefit of the morning sun and its association with Surya, the lord of the sun, who brings us inspiration and enlightenment. This makes the eastern direction ideal for individuals with a propensity or preference for contemplative or scholarly activities. A north-facing home receives the blessings of Soma and Kuber, the lords of health and wealth, respectively, who reside in the north. The north also receives the benefit of the pre-dawn hour and the earliest moments of the rising sun as it casts its delicate rays across the northeast of the house. According to yogis, the pre-dawn hour is the best time for meditation. The west, which belongs to the realm of Varuna, the lord or darkness and the unknown, is relatively peaceful. It does you no harm.

Some current vastu experts believe that you should not live in a home that faces south, since south is the realm of Yama, the god of death, but others insist that since Yama also represents dharma (duty and responsibility), even a south-facing home is acceptable. Mayamata, the ancient vastu treatise, says: "In a house with one single main building, this may be to the east, south, west or north, and is appropriate for all classes."[22] So, don't get overly concerned about the orientation of your site or home; concentrate on the other aspects of vastu living that are more important to put into practice.

SHAPE OF THE SITE AND HOME

The "ideal" shape of piece of land and a house is a square or rectangle. The square, as we've seen, is the Vedic shape that symbolizes the cosmos. It is perceived as the perfect form. If the site is irregular in shape, just mark out

---

[22] Kapila Vatsyayan, general ed. and Bruno Dagens, trans., *Mayamata Vol. 1* (Delhi: Indira Gandhi National Centre for the Arts in association with Motilal Banarsidass Publishers, 1994).

a square and rectangle on the site and use that as your area for development. If your home is L-shaped or split-level, divide the home on the vastu purusha mandala into distinct quadrangles and evaluate the building from the point of view of each separate quadrangle. See the diagrams in Creating Your Spiritual Blueprints, p.102. Circles are dynamic forms and the energy is in constant movement. Such energy can be too extreme to handle and not conducive to inner peace in a home.

FLOW OF ENERGY

You'll remember from school that the earth spins on a north-south axis that tilts to the northeast. The northeast, which is the gateway to the gods, is a major source of positive cosmic energy. The east, ruled by Surya, is the realm of the sun and enlightenment. For this reason, the ideal vastu plot would slope to the north and east and rise to the south and the west, with an actual barrier (a fence, a rock garden, a cluster of trees, a dense hedge) in the southwest.

If there is a depression or a pool or a pond located in the northeast, which belongs to the element of water, so much the better. The presence of a northeastern "receptacle" draws in the energy, which then moves in an arc to the southwest and radiates to the southeast and northwest. A barrier in the southwest, which belongs to the element of earth, helps to hold in the energy so that it keeps flowing around the property. A good barrier can be anything heavy and with height.

LOCATION OF THE HOUSE ON THE SITE

The greatest amount of open land on your site should be left on the east and north, and the house should be set back in the south and west so that your home will receive a greater amount of eastern sun and the positive energy that comes from the northeast. If you are able to choose a location for a garage, choose the southeast or northwest. Your car uses electricity and fuel—heat elements. The element of fire is in the southeast. Because your car also comes and goes, the garage can also work in the northwest, the quadrant of air and movement.

WELCOMING DOOR

An entrance on the north wall of the northeast quadrant of the building allows the positive energy, which comes from the northeast, to flow into your house. An entrance on the east wall fills your home with inspiration and enlightenment. A southern entrance reminds you of your responsibilities. A western entrance speaks of the calm of night and is essentially neutral. Ancient vastu guidelines say that the door to a residence should not be located at the precise center of a cardinal direction, because such placement is restricted to religious institutions.[23] For a home, it is better to have the door to the left or right of the center point of the northern, southern, eastern, or western point on a wall.

INTERIOR LAYOUT

ENHANCING POSITIVE ENERGIES

Because positive energy, which enters through the gateway of the gods in the northeast, travels in an arc to the southwest of the home, try not to disturb this energy flow. If possible, keep the northeast corner in the home and the northeast corner of each room empty of furniture, at least heavy furniture that can stop the circulation of the energy. Keep lightweight furniture

---

[23] Kapila Vatsyayan, general ed. and Bruno Dagens, trans., *Mayamata Vol. 1* (Delhi: Indira Gandhi National Centre for the Arts in association with Motilal Banarsidass Publishers, 1994).

in the north and the east of the home and in the north and the east of each room or wall-less space that serves a specific function in a one-room studio or loft.

To trap this positive energy inside the home, put your heavy furniture in the south and the west of the home and in the south and west of each room or wall-less space. And, if you can afford it, why not consider elevating the floor in the southwest quadrant of the house or living room? Such an elevation in this quadrant, which belongs to the element of earth, makes the area even heavier, thus trapping more positive energy. A raised floor can also be quite dramatic.

FURNITURE PLACEMENT

The proper placement of furniture is extremely important to vastu living. First, keep all furniture, such as desks, beds, sofas, bureaus, and chairs, at least four inches from the wall. This gap prevents your own energies from being absorbed into the wall. Because built-ins, such as cupboards and book-shelves, are incorporated into the wall, consider them part of the wall and just be certain that your desk or chair or any furniture is placed four inches away. More than likely, this gap is already there, so that you can get to these storage areas.

When you create seating arrangements in your home, think about the placement of chairs in particular. If you want everyone to feel comfortable, then be certain that there is at least one chair, in its own inviting environment, that doesn't suggest exclusion but a safe haven for that private person who doesn't want to be right in the thick of things.

To create a convivial atmosphere, make certain that seating arrangements invite conversation. Try this test when a friend comes to visit. Sit side by side and talk. If either of you leans toward the other to participate in the conversation or has to adjust the placement of the chair, then the chairs are too far away or at the wrong angle to reinforce socialization. Incorrect chair arrangement can make the extrovert or introvert, who reside in some measure within us all, feel uncomfortable, ill at ease, and even isolated.

PUT THE ACCENT ON LESS

Did you ever realize that a room can create a feeling of claustrophobia? This is true. The most inviting rooms keep space for your personality and the personality of others. Clutter is not just overbearing; it stifles creativity, spontaneity, even conversation. When you are about to make a purchase for your home, always stop and ask yourself: do I really need this? Does this complement my personality? Will it really fit into the character of the space? Will it create a closed in feeling?

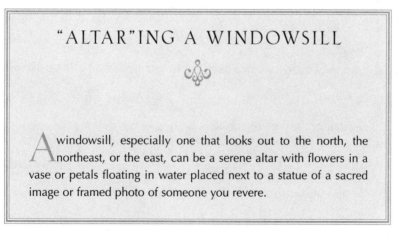

"ALTAR"ING A WINDOWSILL

A windowsill, especially one that looks out to the north, the northeast, or the east, can be a serene altar with flowers in a vase or petals floating in water placed next to a statue of a sacred image or framed photo of someone you revere.

123

AIM FOR FIFTY PERCENT OR BETTER

Finally, do not get discouraged when you begin to put vastu living into practice in your home, especially if you live in the city, where, for most of us, our budget, not the orientation of the rooms inside the space, determines where we live. In most homes, it is difficult, if not impossible, to get everything to conform to all the guidelines. So, once again, aim for fifty percent. If you can meet this level of success, you are doing great. When you do have to go against the guidelines—perhaps you simply have to cover the center space, or the northeast corner of a room is blocked by your dream grand piano—turn to Chapter 9, *Appeasing the Gods—Appeasing Your Soul*. Just select a symbolic solution to appease the gods and symbolically address the disturbance of the harmony among the elements.

PROTECT YOUR ENERGIES

Furniture, except for cabinetry, shelves, or counters that are built into a wall, should be four inches from the wall.

ROOM BY ROOM

THE KITCHEN

FIGURE 33

*Vastu
Kitchen
Layout*

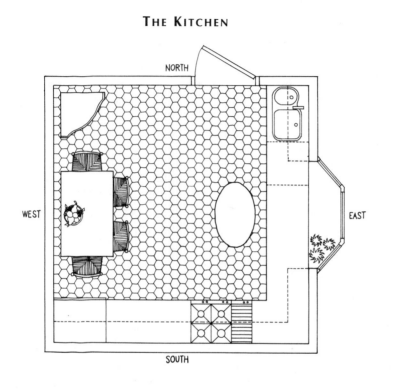

Orientation

Normally, it is best if the kitchen is located in the southeast quadrant, which is the realm of fire. But this may be another space where you would be wise to consider the dominant element in your constitution and think about the rule: like increases like. If you have a pitta (fire) constitution and spend a good part of the day in the kitchen, its placement in the southeast could aggravate your constitution. See Chapter 4, *Vastu and the Vedic View of Health*, for details. You may benefit from a kitchen in the northeast of your home. The northeast quadrant, which is the gateway to the gods, belongs to the element of water. The water element can help maintain the balance in a pitta constitution.

The southwest quadrant is never a good place for the kitchen. Because of the heavy-duty appliances associated with the kitchen and the heat produced by the stove, the kitchen is related to fire. The southwest quadrant bears the sun's intensity. Heat naturally collects in this part of the house. When the kitchen is also in this quadrant, it creates an example of like increasing like. There is too much fire in the southwest quadrant.

If your kitchen ends up in a quadrant other than the southeast, restore the harmony between the elements with a symbolic appeasement. See Chapter 9, *Appeasing the Gods—Appeasing Your Soul*.

Preparing Food

The food preparation area of your kitchen should allow you to face east. Facing east and letting the sun shine on our ingredients makes for healthier food. Without the sun, life on earth would come to an end. Spiritually, when we prepare food while we face the east, we are also paying tribute to Surya, the sun god and sustainer of life.

Appliance Placement

The oven, microwave, and drier, which radiate heat, should be near the southeast corner on the south wall or east wall. The dishwasher and washing machine, which create heat and use water, should be on the east wall in between the northeast and southeast quadrants, so that these appliances receive the benefit of the elements of water in the northeast and the element of fire in the southeast.

The sink should be against the east wall or north wall, near the northeast quadrant, which belongs to the element of water. The refrigerator, which is typically heavy and can trap energy inside the room and home, should be placed against a wall in the south or west. If it is placed in the west, the door also opens to the east, which is good for food.

Furniture Placement

If your kitchen is large enough to accommodate an eating table, try not to place it in the direct center of the room or kitchen space. The center should be kept empty to allow the spiritual power that generates in this area to radiate in all directions. A square or rectangular table is preferable since it has static energy and everyone will be less inclined to eat in a rush, which is not good for digestion. Placing the table directly opposite the eastern wall and a window also allows for the benefit of the morning sun.

Zone of Tranquility

I suggest putting an image or symbolic representation of a deity above the kitchen sink or on the windowsill or shelf above the counter where you prepare meals. You can choose any deity who makes you feel calm or blessed—from Ganesha, the elephant-headed god, to the Buddha. For suggestions, refer to Chapter 9, *Appeasing the Gods—Appeasing Your Soul*. Let this special place be your zone of tranquility. When you are involved in a rhythmic activity—washing dishes, slicing carrots, or ironing, your mind can focus on the image. It will draw you deep inside yourself and reenergize you.

Spice Up Your Kitchen

Spices have a definite place in our kitchen. They add fragrance to the dishes we prepare and fragrance to the air. Spices also play an important role in ayurveda. Cardamom, basil, ginger, cinnamon, coriander, and nutmeg, in particular, are used as infusions or teas to treat various illnesses or to help with digestion, which is often the root cause of many disorders. These spices also give a boost to the mind—helping us to relax, sleep, or feel energetic. Parsley, peppermint, saffron, sandalwood, and turmeric are often used in powder form to cure topical injuries or internal problems.

Spices are used in most Indian dishes, no matter what region of the country—and it's not just because of their flavor. Spices are the jewels of Indian cuisine, adding color and a healthy dose of well-being. When we in the West think of India, we think of curry, and we seem to think curry is a spice. Actually curry is an Anglicized rendering of *kari*, a word for black pepper. Spices appear in numerous dishes, unexpectedly and with great results, such as South Indian curd dishes that are flavored with pepper, ginger, and cinnamon.

To spice up your décor, why not keep dried spices in colorful glass jars or in a spice box? Hang a string of garlic bulbs and use their cloves as often as you can. Garlic is good for your body, especially if you have a sluggish digestion; so just forget about its effect on your breath. If you have a window that receives lots of sun, grow spices or edible flowers (see Chapter 8, *The Gift of Nature*). The garden serves an excellent purpose, providing you with ingredients that are good for your health.

Ambience

The kitchen is one of the most important areas in our home. It is here that we prepare the food for our body's nourishment. We must take care to create a positive ambience that gives us pleasure, so that we willingly spend the required time to prepare our meals. The food that we eat should taste good and look good to the eye. The décor should be soothing, with colors that are gentle and nurturing. Refer to the Color Chart, Harmony in Color on p.198.

A well-designed kitchen is also simple and functional. Try not to clutter it with non–kitchen-oriented items that get in our way or keep us from finding what we need for the preparation of our meals.

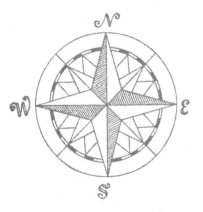

THE DINING ROOM

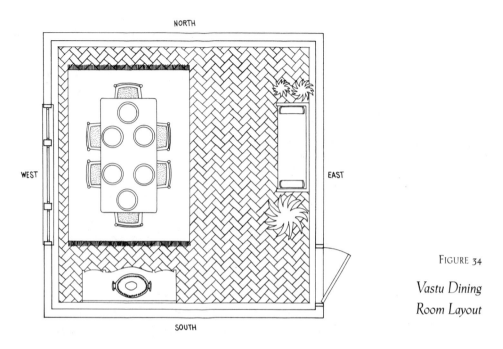

FIGURE 34

*Vastu Dining
Room Layout*

Orientation

The vastu living dining room should be in the western or the eastern side of our home. Obviously, this room should be close to the kitchen.

Furniture Placement

A round or oval dining table creates an abundance of energy. If you want lots of animated conversation at mealtime, you should use one of these shapes. If you prefer a more serene environment during meals, then you should choose a quadrangle, either square or rectangular. Try to avoid placing the table in the center of the room. As you have discovered, the center or Brahmasthana belongs to Brahma and the element of space; it is sacred space. You don't want to trap the spiritual power associated with this area under your feet or under the table. Instead, try placing your dining table toward the western or eastern side of the room. The eastern side can motivate stimulating conversation since this is the direction of enlightenment.

129

The western side is peaceful, signifying the time when darkness and night prevail.

As with all heavy furniture, you should try to put your china cabinet or buffet table at least four inches from the west or south walls. If you have a wine rack, keep it in the north; the healing properties of the north will keep the wine at its best.

Zone of Tranquility

This room can also have a zone of tranquility, which you should try to locate in the north or the east near the northeast corner. A bench with cushions and a small side table can be lovely in a dining room. If you are short on space, think about displaying a photo of someone you respect or hanging a plant, such as holy basil, which is sacred to Vishnu.

Ambience

Often a dining room becomes unintentionally formal, which can reduce or eliminate spontaneity, especially if the formality isn't by choice. Children will clam up, as will your guests. It is healthier to eat in an environment that allows everyone to unwind. To create an informal ambience, keep the lighting soft. Use candles at night or have an overhead light with a dimmer switch so that you can alter the mood. Curtains can also help to create a play of light and shadow during daytime hours. You might try layering them. A good choice would include a transparent layer underneath that can be opened or closed, with an overlayer of heavier drapes in a soft hue or a delicate pattern that can be kept completely open or closed to block out a hot sun and its heat.

A dark pattern in fabric can also increase the feeling of formality. Instead, choose to upholster seats or seat cushions in fabrics that match the cushions on the bench in your zone of tranquility. Also try to mix materials, by using wood with wrought iron, for instance. Wrought iron adds a delicate "airy" touch to a dining room.

And do remember to welcome nature. If you have the space, put a couple of tall leafy plants on the floor.

You can also display a couple of paintings or photographs on the wall or on a table. Photographs of the deceased, however, should be placed in the south and in southwest, which belong to Yama, the lord of death, and Pitri, the lord of ancestors, respectively.

THE LIVING ROOM

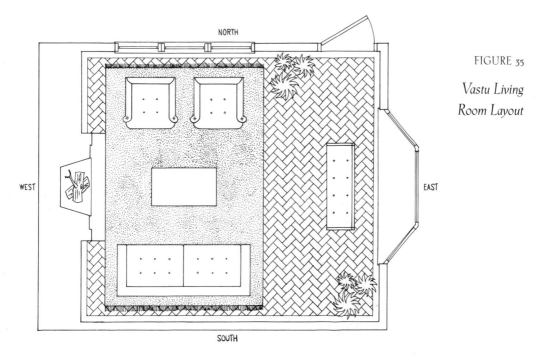

FIGURE 35

Vastu Living Room Layout

Orientation

A good location for the living room is in the northwest, the north, or the northeast of your house.

Northwest

The northwest, which belongs to the element of air, is particularly good if your parties and gatherings tend to run late. People will get restless and move on. This quadrant indicates movement, a characteristic that suits the function of the living room, where people come to visit but don't stay too long.

Northeast

Because the northeast belongs to the element of water, locating your living room in this quadrant will make it a repository of positive cosmic energy. Because the northeast is also the gateway of the gods, you will also find this location serene.

North

A living room in the north puts it in the realm of the two deities, Kuber and Soma. Kuber, the god of wealth and indulgence, loves a good time and will add a congenial ambience. Soma, the god of health, will send wholesome vibrations through the space.

Furniture Placement

You are likely to have many of your heaviest pieces of furniture in your living room. Do your best to put the heaviest pieces in the southern or western part of the space. For example, if you plan to keep books, which are normally heavy, in the living room, try to put built-in bookshelves into the south and west walls, where they will also act as a barrier to keep the positive energy in the room. If you have a large and heavy sofa, this should also be placed in the south or west.

If you have other heavy objects, such as a piano or a heavy wooden storage chest, see if you can put them in this part of the room without creating clutter or an unappealing visual imbalance. You can put some heavy objects in the other areas of the living room or living room space. Just remember: if the vibrations in the room do not feel right, turn to Chapter 9 to find a symbolic gesture to appease the gods.

If you're addicted to television and plan to have a set in this room, here's your remedy: place the television in the northwest corner. The quadrant of air and movement will make you restless and you'll want to turn off the set. Otherwise, place the television and entertainment center in the southeast, the quadrant that belongs to the element of fire.

Zone of Tranquility

If you love to relax in your living room, place your favorite chair in the north or the east near the northeast corner. This way it can double as your zone of tranquility, which can be enhanced with a couple of plants on the floor or a side table with a bowl of shells or pebbles that are soothing to the touch. Or hang an Indian-style swing that creates calming movement as you sway back and forth near a window along the eastern wall.

FIGURE 36

Indian Swing

You could also create a zone of tranquility near a fireplace where the flickering flames create a soothing rhythm that empties your mind of thoughts.

Once again, seating arrangements in this room or space should encourage easy conversation. A coffee table should not be in the direct center of the room, which ought to be open to Brahma. Left empty, the center can circulate spiritual power.

Creating Rhythm

If you add mementos, photographs, or paintings that speak of the past and the present and give a hint to the future, you are reminding us of the rhythm attached to life. Here's your best bet: photos of ancestors belong in the south and southwest, the realm of death and ancestors. Other pictures can be placed in all the other directions. A good way to suggest this rhythm is to group the pictures by generation, placing photos of children on the west wall so that they face east, the direction of enlightenment, and photos of the older generations, but not the deceased, in the north, which represents health and wealth. Another way to honor the ongoing cycle of life is to add an heirloom or something old to a modern decor or add something modern to a traditional and antique-dominated decor.

You can also create rhythm, which connects this space to the rest of the home and you, by featuring parts of a collection that continues from room to room. But don't clutter the living room with furniture that does not serve a specific function. Too much furniture and too much "stuff" in a living room are distracting and create a sense of claustrophobia.

Ambience

An ideal living room is friendly and welcoming—a space that invites everyone to relax and feel at home. Help this space live up to its name. It should vibrate in consonance with the vibrations of the occupants of the home. You want your guests to enter this room and enjoy it as much as they enjoy your company. Add more life to the room by incorporating some elements from the natural world: plants, clay pots, stone sculptures. Even if you prefer to have a formal decor, don't allow that decision to result in a room without warmth. Lighting and the use of curtains can also do a lot for the ambience.

THE HOME OFFICE OR STUDY

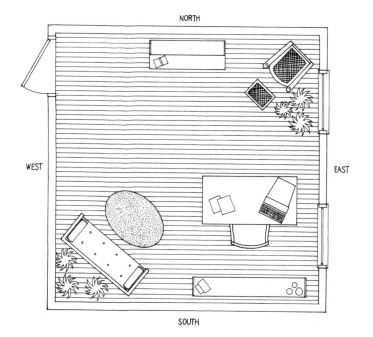

FIGURE 37

*Vastu Home
Office or
Study Layout*

More and more people have started to work at home instead of, or in addition to, going off to an office. I'm sure this trend will continue; it's part of the freedom that comes from e-mail, cell phones, pagers, and fax and scan machines. We're entering the flexibility-in-work age and the era of contracted work. A good number of us enjoy working for ourselves because it gives us a greater degree of control over our working conditions and therefore our feelings about our work.

If you work at home, you probably spend a lot of time in your workspace, maybe as much as you do in your bedroom. Therefore, you'll want to think carefully about the orientation of this room, the furniture placement, and its ambience. This space needs to fit us just right and it should not have a negative impact on your particular constitution. Your home workspace should be soothing, inspiring, and fill your soul with positive energy so that you can do good work. If you don't work at home but have a study, you'll still want to attain the same objectives—creating a room that you enjoy.

Orientation

A home office or study should be placed in the east, the north, or the west of your home. The east is a particularly good choice since it is the direction of inspiration and enlightenment. Locating an office or study in the northwest, which belongs to the element of air, is likely to make you restless, unfocused and indecisive. You may even find yourself absent from your job if you chose this location for your home office or study.

Furniture Placement

The ideal location for your desk is in the south or west—this is especially important if the desk is heavy. If you want to reinforce the qualities of strength, leadership, power, and decisiveness, try to sit in the south, the realm of earth and heaviness. And when you sit in the south, you should face north or northeast. The north brings you health and wealth. The northeast brings you serenity from the element of water and positive cosmic energy. If you place your desk in the west and face east, this leads to contemplation, creativity, inspiration, and focus.

All heavy items, such as bookcases and file cabinets and sofas, should be kept in the south or the west. If you want to study well or work well, it is unwise to put a television in this space. It will serve as a distraction. If you must have one in your study or office, then put it in the restless realm of the northwest where you are most likely to get distracted and turn it off. A music system and computer can be in the southeast. Don't forget to keep empty the sacred center to allow the spiritual power to radiate through the room and toward your soul.

Zone of Tranquility

A zone of tranquility would work well in the north, the northeast, or the east of this room or space. These directions are inspirational and positive. Place a lightweight wicker chair that allows you to sit back and relax in the northeast—the gateway to the gods—and let the positive energy flow over you as you free your self from all thoughts. The zone can also be unobtrusive—something small, such as a small statue of a deity or a tribute to a dis-

136

play of natural objects. When you are working at your desk, you can pause and reflect on the symbolism that exists in this quiet zone.

Ambience

If you are using this room or space as an office, think of it as a peaceful study. Why? Because work in our world has the power to take over our lives. While it is necessary for a successful home office to create an ambience that is conducive to productive work, this space must also remind us that life is more than punching a personal time clock. Our work should help us move through life; we should enjoy it and grow from our work experiences. But we should never let work balloon out of proportion.

A rounded life that feeds the soul is a healthy life. We must love ourselves even as we work. We must remember that every room in the home, including a home office, is supposed to be a spiritual refuge for the body. So the ambience in our home office must approach that of a study—reflective and enlightening. It should beckon us to enter. It should create a feeling that allows us to be contemplative, curious, and open-minded, ready to absorb new information. Finally, this special room should remind us of our soul's connection to the spiritual side of existence. This will help us eliminate a lot of the stress that feeds off a soulless work environment.

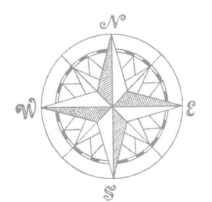

THE ZONE OF TRANQUILITY

FIGURE 38

*Vastu Zone
of Tranquility
Layout*

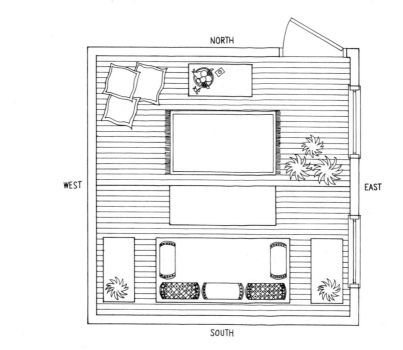

Orientation

As you have seen, you can create zones of tranquility in any room. As long as you are assured of some private space for reflection and tranquility somewhere in your home, then you don't need a separate room for your zone of tranquility. This zone only needs to be large enough for you to relax in comfort, to sit cross-legged in the lotus position, to lie down on your back and close your eyes, or to practice yoga.

If you do have the space and the inclination to create a spiritual room devoted to yoga or meditation or pure relaxation, its ideal location is in the northeast, the east, or the north of your home. If the space has a window looking to the east or northeast, this creates a spiritually charged room. You have the advantage of the gateway to the gods with its positive energy, and in the east you have the advantage of inspiration.

Furniture Placement

The zone of tranquility should have a minimum amount of furniture. If you are able to sit low to the floor, place a mattress in the south, the south-west, or the west of the space so that you can face east or northeast when you meditate. You should also face east when you do asanas (body postures).

Place a low table on either side of the floor mattress and create an altar with the deity facing the east or the north or just use its symbolic representation (see Chapter 9, *Appeasing the Gods—Appeasing Your Soul*). Include the presence of each element on the altar: a small clay vessel (earth) with water and a candle that you light when you are in the room (fire). The flicker of the flame represents air. Create a small sacred empty center (space) on this table.

This is one space that really needs a large empty center or Brahmasthana so that the spiritual power radiates freely in every direction. Use nature to bring more life into the décor and place live plants or cut flowers in the north or the east. Choose medicinal or fragrant plants (see Chapter 8, *The Gift of Nature*). Put a music system in the southeast of this room so that you can play soothing music. When you leave this room, turn on a low light. This room should never be left in darkness: the light of enlightenment must always shine.

Ambience

The focus of this room or space should be on the nurturing of your soul and the reaffirmation of your soul's divinity and sacredness. This is where you come to escape the world that makes you feel anything but inner peace. So, everything about this room should evoke positive feelings that soothe you and let you empty your mind. The room should always be clean and free of clutter, which symbolizes disarray and makes you lose your power of concentration.

Your personal zone of tranquility must keep you in touch with all creation. It must quietly remind you of the divinity that you share with all universal forms, including the elements of nature that you might not think about on a daily basis. The objective is to establish a sacred zone that blesses you so much that you look forward to being there. And just your awareness of the presence of this zone in your home should exert a becalming influence.

THE BEDROOMS—GENERAL GUIDELINES

Sleep with your head to the south or the east. The south brings a good deep sleep; the east brings enlightenment to the subconscious. Never sleep with your head to the north. In vastu, the head is considered the North Pole of the body and by sleeping with the head in the direction of the North Pole, the two repel each other. You will not have a restful sleep.

This may come as a surprise, but do be careful about what image you put on the wall at the foot of your bed. It is likely to be the first thing that you see when you awaken. Choose an attractive wall hanging or a picture that brings you pleasure.

If the bedroom has an attached bathroom, always keep the bathroom door closed. Keep closet doors closed and bureau or chest drawers shut tight. Open drawers and doors create a feeling of clutter. If you have a desk in your bedroom, be sure that it is left neat before you retire at night. Clutter can get in the way of a good night's sleep.

Also, try to train yourself to open the windows to air out the room every morning for at least a few minutes. Do this even in the winter; the brief spell of fresh air is refreshing and revitalizing.

Orientation

Because you spend so many hours in your bedroom, you need to think carefully about its location and how it affects your personality and constitution—your pitta (fire), vata (air), or kapha (water) constitution. In general, the bedroom can be in any area of your home, but the preferred locations for bedrooms are the southwest, the west, and the northwest.

If you have a pitta (fire) constitution, you should probably not sleep in the southeast, which is the realm of fire. You would be better off sleeping in the northeast quadrant, the realm of water, which would quiet down your fiery temperament and help you relax. If you have a vata (air) constitution, then you could also try sleeping in the northeast, where the realm of water will have a calming influence, or you could sleep in the southwest, where the earth element is heavy and quiescent. If you have a kapha (water) constitution, try not to sleep in the northeast, the realm of water. These suggestions, again, are based on the rule of like increases like, which could upset your constitution.

If you decide to sleep in the southeast or have no other choice of locations, just be careful not to put your bed near the southeast corner of the room or space. You will be sleeping on too much fire. If you have trouble sleeping and spend a lot of the night tossing and turning, then don't sleep in the northwest quadrant. This quadrant is the realm of air and movement.

A good indication that something is wrong with where you are sleeping is a constant desire to rearrange your bedroom. The problem may not be the arrangement of the furniture, but the location of the room itself. Maybe your children or your guests are sleeping where you should be sleeping. If you have only one bedroom, do be sure to sleep with your head to the east or the south.

Furniture Placement

The bed or beds should not be in the direct center of a bedroom. Place them so that there is more open space on the north and the east. Since the bed is normally a heavy object, it should usually be placed in the south, the southwest, or the west of the room. This is also one piece of furniture that should not touch the wall. Keep it four inches away so that the wall will not disturb your energies while you sleep.

The bedroom may have many other heavy pieces of furniture. If the room is large, then you may have enough space to place the heaviest objects, such as an armoire, wardrobe, or floor-to-ceiling bookcases, in the south, the southwest, or the west of the room, and still maintain visual balance. Lighter pieces, such as a bureau, delicate sofa, or reading chair, can be safely placed in the north, the east, or the northeast of the room.

If you have a desk with a computer, create a study or work area near the southeast wall so that you can sit facing the north, the northeast or east, even while you stare into the computer monitor. These directions are beneficial for you.

It can be difficult, but try to create an open center space even if it is tiny. If the room size makes this impossible and the room does not evoke feelings of comfort, then make an appeasement to the element of space or Brahma (see Chapter 9, *Appeasing the Gods—Appeasing Your Soul*). This will enable you to receive the spiritual power that comes from the sacred center.

The feeling of nature should also circulate through your bedroom so that you feel connected to the larger world and never feel alone. If you don't have enough light for plants, then incorporate organic products into your bedroom: cane wastepaper baskets, dried flower arrangements, potpourri.

You should also place photographs of your family and loved ones in this room—they help define you and add to the room's identity. But do remember that photographs of ancestors or the deceased should be on the south or the west walls near the southwest corner.

Television and stereo systems should be in the southeast of the room, which belongs to the element of fire. Again, if you have a tendency to watch too much television, then place the television in the northwest, which belongs to the element of air with its characteristic of movement. You will become restless and turn off the set. And if you are someone who leaves on your television, music system, or computer overnight, know that this is not a wise idea. The active energy from these electronics can interfere with your sleep and the electrical fields may harm your body.

Zone of Tranquility

A bedroom can have an extremely personalized zone of tranquility, a zone that represents your special identity and connection to the world. As always, this space should be in the north or the east near the northeast corner of the room—the gateway to the gods and the source of positive energy.

Ambience

The bedroom is a private space that should be aesthetically appealing and inviting. Once you enter your bedroom, you want to feel comfortable and secure. This is why the room must reflect the personality and needs of each individual who sleeps here. When you sleep, you surrender, and the room must feel like a protective shelter.

THE MASTER BEDROOM

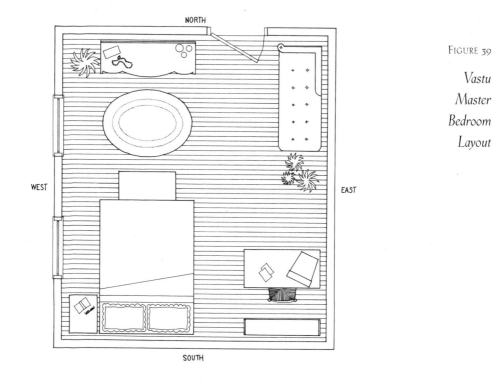

FIGURE 39

*Vastu
Master
Bedroom
Layout*

Orientation

Ideally, the master bedroom should be in the southwest, which is the quadrant of the element of earth and speaks of heaviness and strength. If you are living alone, you can let your personality determine where you sleep. You should also consider the needs of your particular constitution. But if you live with your children and they sleep in the southwest, guess who could try to dominate? To maintain your role as parent, the one who offers guidance and teaches good values, you should sleep in the southwest—not your children.

Furniture Placement

Furniture placement should follow the General Guidelines, Furniture Placement for bedrooms, above (see p.141). Of all rooms, this should certainly reflect your interests and personality. If you are married or have a partner, make your bedroom an intimate space that shows the connection between two people who care about one another.

Zone of Tranquility

If you don't have a separate room or separate space in the home dedicated exclusively to a zone of tranquility, the zone of tranquility in the bedroom should be especially inviting, relaxing, and sheltering. Set up in the north, the northeast, or the east so you can absorb the positive energies, this spiritual place can be discreetly romantic, with the fragrance of fresh flowers or delicate incense. It should honor nature and you.

Ambience

Follow the advice for ambience, under General Guidelines, Ambience for bedrooms, above (see p.142). But here is one special thought for this particular room. Have controlled lighting, romantic music ready to play, attractive candles, and fresh flowers as often as you can afford, so that you enjoy your intimate moments. The expression of love should be celebrated in a beautiful environment.

THE CHILDREN'S BEDROOM

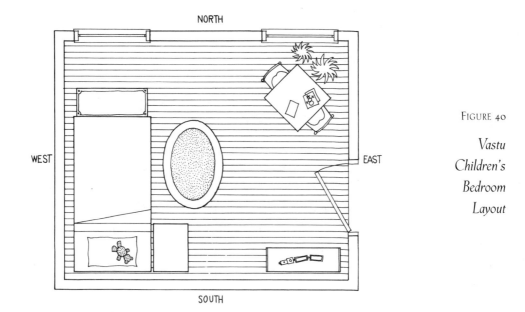

FIGURE 40

*Vastu
Children's
Bedroom
Layout*

Orientation

Your child's bedroom can be in any quadrant in the home, but do keep in mind the problem that can arise when children sleep in the southwest. If you are eager for your grown-up "child" to leave the nest, put this bedroom in the northwest of the home, or put the bed in the northwest corner of a room. The element of air will stir constant thoughts of moving out.

Furniture Placement

Furniture placement should follow the guidelines described above under General Guidelines, Furniture Placement for bedrooms (p.141). A child who has trouble sleeping is apt to get a good night's rest if the head of the bed is in the south. If the head of the bed is in the east, this direction fills a sleeping child with inspiration and enlightenment.

Since a major part of your child's life is engaged in learning and discovery, you should positively and actively reinforce this process. Have a huge bulletin board or an entire wall in the bedroom that showcases your child's work and accomplishments. Each child's bedroom should also have a place to put books.

Zone of Tranquility

Since most children get rambunctious, don't forget a zone of tranquility in the north, the northeast, or the east of the room. And don't make this zone a punishment corner. It should be a place for quiet activities where a child will not be disturbed.

Ambience

Follow the same advice offered above under General Guidelines, Ambience for bedroooms (see p.142) to create the proper ambience. But remember that each child's bedroom should make a child feel worthy and loved. It must nurture your child's mind, sense of self, and soul.

THE GUEST BEDROOM

Orientation

Unless you hate to see your guests leave, let them sleep in the northwest of your home. They will not hang around forever. The element of air will fill them with the urge to move on.

Furniture Placement and Ambience

Again, furniture placement should follow the General Guidelines, Furniture Placement and Ambience for bedrooms, above (p.141 and 142 respectively). Although most guests only come for a short stay, the guest bedroom should never feel like a hotel bedroom. It should be connected to the rest of your home and reflect your personality and interests.

THE BATHROOM

In India, the act of taking a bath is a ritual imbued with sacredness. To get into this healthy habit, train yourself to think of your bathroom as a spiritual space. The bathroom is where you cleanse the body that protects the soul. For starters, only use organic products on your body. It's even easy to create your own products from fresh organic produce. Here are two simple preparations: rest a thin slice of cucumber on each closed eyelid for about five minutes to soothe the eyes while you relax in the bath; mix ground oatmeal and almond oil together to create a healthy scrub for the body.

Bring nature into the bathroom. If the bathroom gets good sun, grow aloe, a natural healing agent for the skin. Each day, break open a small part of a stem and use the juice for a natural astringent. Think about the bath or shower as a time to pamper your body, which, again, is the temple of your soul. Take a leisurely bath. Turn this daily activity into a time to relax and empty your mind of everything but positive thoughts.

Orientation

The bathroom in the east catches the morning sunrays, which feel good on the body. But the bathroom can be located anywhere in the house except the northeast, which is the sacred gateway to the gods. Ideally, medicine should be kept on the northern wall of a bathroom, where they receive the blessings of Soma, the lord of health. The toilet should face the north or the south.

Let the bathtub be your zone of tranquility. Roll up a towel to create a natural bath pillow so that you can recline in comfort. Treat yourself to a healthy and mentally relaxing ten-minute facial with natural products, such as a sticky combination of lemon juice and honey. Men should do this, too. This ten minutes of quiet time spent stretched out in a tub of warm water will empty your mind. Your soul will shine through.

THE TERRACE, BALCONY, PORCH, AND VERANDAH

A terrace, balcony, porch, or verandah serves an important function in relation to the home—one that is usually overlooked. Did you ever think of these places, which are outside but connected to our house, as the link between the exterior world and our private world? When we sit and relax in these areas we place ourselves in the middle zone before we go into the private zone of our home in our life, or go out into the public zone of the exterior world.

Orientation

The preferred locations for a special middle zone are the east, north, and west. The north gives you a taste of the sunrise and sunset. The east is an ideal space for a thinker and an early riser who likes to experience the reawakening of the sun. The west is for individuals whose quiet time is in the early evening. When you sit in the west, serenity enters your soul as you watch the diminishing rays give way to darkness.

Furniture Placement

A porch swing, a hanging swing, hanging chairs—furniture that provides gentle movement—create a predictable rhythm that lets the mind wander. We relax. A swing should be placed so that it takes in the best view and also allows a bit of privacy so that it can serve as a zone of tranquility. All furniture should celebrate natural materials, not plastic, and be grouped for quiet conversation. If there is sufficient sun, surround yourself with plants: window boxes, plants in containers on the floor, hanging plants on wall brackets or hooks from a ceiling (if there is one).

Ambience

A middle zone should create a harmonious transition that blends nature, which represents the outside zone, with personal comforts, which reflect the private zone of the home. This harmony should establish a comfortable and secure ambience. We should feel compelled to linger and just enjoy watching the views and listening to the sounds around us.

PUTTING THE DIVINE IN THE DÉCOR

According to vastu, the home is a temple for the body and soul. The objects that surround you and the way that they are arranged in every room should reinforce this premise. A vastu home, appropriately decorated, makes you feel good.

BOOKS

Books may be a statement of our personal interests and speak of our inner self, so it is best to keep books tidy and in some order. A sloppy bookcase that becomes a home for whatever fits shows disrespect for a book collection and perhaps for ourselves. A bookcase where books are arranged by subject or category might make you inclined to choose to look at a title if you like books and are curious. But a bookcase where the tops of books have become shelves themselves, or where the front space of every inch of bookshelf has become a parking lot for more than loose change makes most people not want to touch a book at all. Since reading is often a hoarded, good pleasure, offer yourself and your friends access to your books.

CARPETS AND TILES

Terra cotta or stone tiles that peek around the perimeters of an area rug add an earthy tone to a room. Vegetable-dye colors in rugs honor the agricultural aspects of nature, the colors seen in the woods and in the fields. The careful choice of floor coverings gives a lovely and personal touch to a home. Wall-to-wall carpeting, functional as it is, is less appealing and less evocative. Try, if you can, to avoid such carpeting. It will cover the floor, but little else. Wall-to-wall carpeting does not express anything about us, except

149

perhaps the need to muffle noise, or to cover a really bad floor or to protect us from a winter chill.

FLOWERS

Flowers always please us. Their fragrance, if there is fragrance, is usually most delightful and evocative. The colors and delicacy and extraordinary diversity, even from flower to flower within a plant, can take hours to absorb. Their presence in the home is such a forceful reminder of nature's beauty. And that feeling of beauty originates in our soul. It is rare that a Hindu temple, where puja (worship) goes on, lacks flowers as a gift presented to the deity. Present yourself with flowers, and celebrate your connection to the world and the Supreme Creator. For variety, try floating flower blossoms or petals in a shallow clay bowl.

HEIRLOOMS

Family heirlooms (from a grandfather clock or hope chest to small precious mementos) belong in the south or the southwest of a room. Their presence in this area devoted to death and ancestors will link us to their wisdom and remind us of the natural cycle of life. To look at the past and study the images of departed loved ones causes us to search for the links that binds us to them. We think of them and imagine that they are still with us on a deep level that communicates with our soul.

MIRRORS—THE LOOK-OUT GLASS

Many Hindus rely on mirrors embedded into a front door to deflect bad luck from the home. If there isn't a mirror on the entrance door, you will often see a mirror, which serves the same function, as soon as you enter the home. Beautiful mirrors are available everywhere, modern and antique; but to promote tranquility, choose polygon shapes. A circle can release too much energy.

MUSICAL INSTRUMENTS

It is wonderful to surround yourself with musical instruments, but they need loving care. If an instrument is on display, make certain that it is out of harm's way. Except for instruments with pedals, other instruments should avoid contact with a person's foot. Bumping an instrument with your foot is a sign of disrespect.

Remember that instruments perform a great service for us. The well-loved instrument can make music that lifts our spirits or makes us laugh, puzzles us, astounds us, or moves us into deep meditation. We should also treat our human voice with care. It is generally not good to shout or scream. We can learn to give all sources of sound the same respect that one offers to God. Remember: it was the primordial sound AUM and its vibration that gave rise to creation.

PAINTINGS AND PHOTOGRAPHS

Paintings, pictures, and photographs should be a positive force. Yes, we may have pictures of someone we love who is dead, but the memories of that person are still a source of great comfort. Please keep your pictures of ancestors in the south or southwest, the realms of ancestors and death. Don't put pictures of ancestors in the zone of tranquility; this area should be about the present, to train ourselves to focus on the now. Pictures or photographs that inspire us or fill us with respect should be located in the north, the east, or the west.

151

TV OR NOT TV

Never let the television and the entertainment center become the social heart of a room. The television is not conducive to socializing and it is not the heart or soul of anything. Television can be educating, but it is normally a passive way to spend time. There are two important places in any room: that special area where people can focus on one another, and the zone of tranquility that turns the focus inward and onto the soul.

BLESSINGS OVERHEAD

FIGURE 41

Indian Toran

The Indian *toran* is a lovely overhead decoration that sanctifies the home and reinforces the nature of the godliness within us and within our personal domain. The toran, which is often seen in the home, is frequently created out of embroidered and mirror-work fabric and hung over the interior of the entrance door. The toran brings good luck and blessings to the occupants and anyone who enters the home. It is a gesture full of kindness and reverence.

VALUABLES

Kuber, the lord of wealth, is in the north. This is the direction where vastu says we should hide all our wealth. Thieves would have a field day if we all followed this rule in our home. But we can put our "invaluable" valuables, those irreplaceable possessions, in the north—the clay sculptures made by our children in elementary school, an embroidered work made by our mother, folkart that reflects the world's diversity. A book that gives you great comfort can be worth more than a rare first edition. Expensive material possessions are not as important as memories that celebrate a life built around noble values.

7

VASTU LIVING AT WORK

Nothing turns out right so long as there is no harmony between body, mind and soul.

—MAHATMA GANDHI

SPIRITUALITY AT WORK

ACCORDING TO THE Vedic texts, the divine exists within us all, within the building as well as in the external environment. And yet spirituality is rarely honored in the Western workspace. At best, a spiritual life is treated the same as a lunch break or workout at the gym. It is an activity crammed into stolen time.

Most of us don't even consider the workspace as a part of us. We don't claim it as our space in the way that we claim our homes. We think of work as a place where we "must" spend our time—and we derive pleasure to the extent that the time passes quickly and is generally free of turbulence. Rushing through work, however, often robs us of the pleasure that comes with the discovery of the solution to a difficult problem. The goal to finish whatever-now-no-matter-what consumes people, and strips work of meaning. It can also lead to mistakes.

These days, with more and more people working in cubicles and wall-less offices, it can be a real challenge to introduce vastu living to one's workspace. Quarters can be so cramped that one is even unable to find the Brahmasthana, the sacred center space. The lack of natural sunlight, openable windows, and the invisible presence of recycled, temperature-controlled air eliminate anyone's ability to experience the natural rhythm of the earth. It is a challenge to do good work in a bad environment.

Fortunately, vastu can put us on the right track to reversing whatever negativity churns around the workspace. It can help us turn our workspaces into friendly spaces, introducing energies that celebrate life. By slowing us down, vastu helps us overcome the problems that come with being in near-constant overdrive. Because vastu living underscores the importance of mutual respect, it can help foster a strong harmonious relationship between you and your colleagues and between you and the elements in your workspace. Bringing vastu principles into the workspace gives you a wonderful new opportunity to find satisfaction in your work, whatever it is.

CLAIM YOUR WORKSPACE

Please, please don't ever view your workspace as temporary space that doesn't belong to you. It is your space. It is where you work, so claim it for yourself. Yes, you may end up moving to another post within your company or taking another job elsewhere, but this is where you are working now and you must treat it with care. If you put vastu into your space, it will nurture you. The best first step you can take is to train your mind to think of your workspace as sacred.

CLAIM YOUR WORK

I cannot overemphasize the importance of learning how to work for your own satisfaction, not for the satisfaction of your boss or your company. Once you make this shift and begin to work for yourself, you will most likely find pleasure in your work—no matter what the work. You will also do better work. When you work for yourself, it is difficult to accept anything less than your best effort. Learning to believe that your work is your own is the second most important step that you can take toward vastu living.

HARMONY AND RHYTHM

As in your home, it is necessary to create harmony between the elements and you and your workspace. Harmony is a prerequisite to inner peace (yes, it is possible to find inner peace at work!). You can, for example, bring the rhythm of life into your personal workspace by creating a square photomontage that chronicles your growth, the growth of your child, your partner, your best friends. The square signifies the universe and the harmonious balance within the universe. Hang it on a wall where you can easily see it during the course of your day.

Even in a windowless cubicle, you can take advantage of the soothing and positive influence of nature. If you happen to have a window with sunlight or decent overhead lighting, you can introduce live plants. If you don't get much natural sunlight, try bouquets of fresh or dried flowers or other organic products, such as small wood or rattan boxes. Or put down an inexpensive jute area rug or a *dhurrie* (woven rug of cotton or wool or camel hair) or *kilim* (a woven tapestry rug). Even visitors and co-workers will feel comfortable when they enter your space.

MAKE ROOM FOR PEACE AND SERENITY

Try to create an area for calm and reflection: a zone of tranquility. Even if you work in the tiniest cubicle or office, you can dedicate a small space to a shallow vase with flower petals floating on water or a glass jar filled with glistening pebbles, or a terra cotta dish filled with sand and seashells that are soothing to touch, or whatever pleases you, including your pet rock. Your zone of tranquility should evoke for you the beauty of creation and the eternal presence of spiritual power. What could be better for defusing stress in the middle of a tense day?

Your zone of tranquility should be so appealing that you can look at it and clear your head whenever you are frustrated. Help yourself to a tranquility break, perhaps instead of a coffee break. You can recharge by focusing on nothing but your breathing for five minutes, which is superior to a recharge on caffeine. It works. You'll return to work with positive energy, not just coffee jitters.

HONOR THE DIVINE ESSENCE

Once you create a space dedicated to tranquility, work cannot overcome you. During the course of your moments of reflection, you will probably discover or remember, sooner or later, that your work or your career does not define you. Work is an important part of us all, but it is not *all* of us. What matters most is you: your unique being, a divine part of the Supreme Creator.

ORIENTATION AND SHAPE

PLEASE NOTE: If you live in the southern hemisphere, you will need to shift everything on the vastu purusha mandala 90 degrees to the right. For example, any advice that suggests the northeast would mean the southeast in the southern hemisphere.

CARDINAL DIRECTIONS

NORTH

DEITY:
Soma and Kuber

IDENTIFICATION:
Health and Wealth

WEST

DEITY:
Varuma

IDENTIFICATION:
Unknown and Darkness

EAST

DEITY:
Surya

IDENTIFICATION:
Enlightenment and Inspiration

SOUTH

DEITY:
Yama

IDENTIFICATION:
Death, Duty, and Responsibility

INTERMEDIATE DIRECTIONS

NORTHWEST

ELEMENT:
Air

DEITY:
Vayu

NORTHEAST

ELEMENT:
Water

DEITY:
Isa

CENTER

ELEMENT:
Space

DEITY:
Brahma

SOUTHWEST

ELEMENT:
Earth

DEITY:
Pitri

SOUTHEAST

ELEMENT:
Fire

DEITY:
Agni

SHAPE OF THE SITE AND WORK SPACE

The site and the workspace should be rectangular or square; most people work more comfortably in a space that conforms to one of these shapes. Quadrangles have static energy, are conducive to thinking, and are relatively easier to turn into a becalming environment. Circular and oval spaces, which are dynamic and charged with moving energy, are fine for sports arenas, where action defines the game.

FLOW OF ENERGY

If you are choosing a site for a company or personal office, remember the importance of attracting and trapping the positive cosmic energies. If there is a slope on the property, it ideally should lead down to the north and the east. These two quadrants should also bear less weight and a minimum of construction so that the positive energy, which enters from the northeast corner, the heavenly gateway and the realm of water, are unobstructed and free to move through the site. When you leave more open area in the north and east, you also receive maximum morning sun. Northern light is called the painter's steady light.

A natural depression in the northeast or a pond or fountain is a plus. The lowland acts as a receptacle that collects the positive energy. The optimum site should also be higher and heavier in the south and in the west so that the cosmic energies, which travel in a diagonal arc from the northeast to the southwest (the element of earth), are trapped inside the property.

ENTRANCE DOOR

Two locations of the entrance door are most likely to reduce workspace stress: the north and the east close to the northeast corner. The northeast corner is the heavenly gateway that draws in the positive energy. It is also the location of the element of water, which is calming. As with the home, the entrance door to a company building should not be located in the exact center of a cardinal direction. Ideally, the correct placement of the door is to the left or right of the center point of the northern wall, the southern wall, the eastern wall, or the western wall. But since the majority of us obviously can't make structural changes to the company building, we should focus our attention on other vastu guidelines that we have the power to control. If you really *feel* that an improperly located door is the source of your stress, don't despair. You can correct the problem with a symbolic solution. See Chapter 9, *Appeasing the Gods—Appeasing Your Soul*.

INVENTORY EXIT

If you sell products, place your inventory in the northwest, which belongs to the element of air. In this quadrant, with its characteristic of movement, the inventory moves out quickly. We use this same principle at home by having our guests sleep in the northwest. In the case of a business, a fast-moving inventory is the key to success.

INTERIOR LAYOUT

CORRIDORS AND PASSAGEWAYS

If possible, keep the passageways wider in the north and east of the workspace. Passageways should also be kept reasonably empty and free of heavy furniture or heavy equipment so that the positive energy that enters from the northeast can move easily through the space.

INTERIOR DOORS

Since stress can invade the workspace, the optimum direction for an entrance door is near the northeast corner, which receives positive energy and represents the soothing element of water. The doors inside the work place should not be located at the precise center of a cardinal direction. See Entrance Door, above (p.159). Again, if you can't make structural changes, you can consider a corrective remedy in Chapter 9, *Appeasing the Gods—Appeasing Your Soul*.

WINDOWS AND BALCONIES AND TERRACES

Taking maximum advantage of the morning sunlight that comes through eastern windows is wise. Farmers know that plants grow best in the morning's east light. Windows in the west and the south should have heavy drapes with transparent undercurtains, or blinds, or shutters that permit you to control the intensity of the afternoon sun.

Gentle colors and organic materials work best for window shades. Wooden shutters or blinds made out of wood slats, jute, linen, or crushed silk bring nature into the workspace. If you have a balcony or a terrace, the place of honor belongs to nature with potted shrubs or trees if the light is good. Otherwise, use chairs made of natural products. Shun plastic. It does harm to our environment. If you have a window, you might put a plant you like on the sill, but don't forget to feed and water it.

THE SACRED CENTER

The center of every space should be clean, and empty. This is the realm of Brahma. Spiritual power emanates from the sacred center of a room, radiating in every direction. If you can arrange your workspace like a temple, with the center space as the inner sanctum that protects you and the deity Brahma, you will thrive on the results.

ZONE OF TRANQUILITY

A zone of tranquility is essential in every workspace. Remember this is not the same as the sacred center. Whether you work on your own or for a company, this zone will provide a calming influence, beneficial to your work. The ideal location for this special space is in the north, the northeast, or the east. In the north, you receive the blessings from Kuber, the lord of wealth, and Soma, the lord of health—all of which adds up to healthy finances. In the northeast, you face the gateway of the gods, which gives you positive energy. In the east, you are the beneficiary of light and enlightenment, and the morning sun if you have a window.

Although many companies now provide employees with on-site day care, a canteen or cafeteria, and even a health club or gym, few think of the need for a calm and quiet space. Smart administrators would provide a special area where employees can take a "health break" and listen to contemplative music while they meditate, do yoga, or just sit back and close their eyes. A company would reap benefits from this in increased productivity and so would we.

DRINKING WATER AND BATHROOM

Drinking fountains and coolers should be near the northeast corner, the direction controlled by the element of water. Bathrooms can be located in any quadrant but the northeast, because waste would pollute the sacred water element. Toilets ought to be placed in the direction of the south or the north.

WHERE TO SIT AT WORK

When you sit at your desk, ideally you should face the east, the northeast, or the north. East is a smart choice since it is the direction of enlightenment, and is thus ideal for creative work, from writing and composing to inventing software programs and inventing anything else. These activities demand a lot of inspiration. The northeast, the gateway to the gods, increases positive energy. The north honors the gods of wealth and health, both of which we all need. You should place the desk, however, in the south or west near the southwestern quadrant, which is the realm of the element of earth and ancestors, who endow this quadrant with wisdom and strength. This location is extremely good for people who are leaders or who are developing leadership and decision-making skills.

FURNITURE AND EQUIPMENT PLACEMENT

With the exception of built-in furniture, keep equipment and furniture at least four inches from the wall. This empty space prevents your own energies from being absorbed into the wall behind you or in front of you. Put light furniture in the north and east. Try to avoid putting any heavy or tall object in the northeast corner that could obstruct the positive energy. The northeast is also the best location for a zone of tranquility. Place heavy furniture and heavy industrial equipment in the south and the west. Their weight serves as a barrier that keeps the positive energies inside your workspace. If your company or personal work requires the use of heavy-duty electrical equipment, put this equipment in the southeast, the realm of the element of fire. Circuit breakers should also be placed in this quadrant.

Don't forget that furniture placement can also improve your physical constitution—pitta (fire), vata (air), and kapha (water). These constitutions, which relate to the elements in our body, are connected to ayurveda, the science of life. See Chapter 4, *Vastu and the Vedic View of Health.* Because you spend so many hours at work, where you sit and even the location of your office can have a strong influence on your health. Always try to follow the sensible rule: like increases like. For example, if you have a pitta (fire) constitution, it may be wise for you to avoid working in the southeast, which is the realm of fire. You may feel better if you work in the northeast. This quadrant, which belongs to the element of water, will cool down your fire.

163

If you have a kapha (water) constitution, you should probably avoid working in the northeast quadrant, the realm of water. It could be far healthier for you to have your personal workspace in one of the southern quadrants, which will not aggravate your kapha constitution. If you have a vata (air) constitution, then you probably shouldn't work in the northwest, the realm of air. Instead consider working in the quadrants that belong to the elements of water or earth. These elements will not interfere with your constitution. If you have no control over where you work on the company premises, then at least try to sit in a quadrant within your space that is healthy for your constitution.

You can apply all this advice when you sit or relax—in the conference room, in a company canteen or company cafeteria, or when you go out to eat.

AIM FOR 50 PERCENT OR BETTER

Also, remember that you will reap the benefits of vastu living if you can incorporate even just 50 percent of the vastu living guidelines. This is an important reminder since many workspaces have problems that are far beyond our control. If you recognize a problem that you cannot resolve without getting fired, and you know that it interferes with your work, make an appeasement. This allows you to reinstate the essential harmony with the element and its deity (see Chapter 9, *Appeasing the Gods—Appeasing Your Soul*).

ROOM BY ROOM

RECEPTION AREA

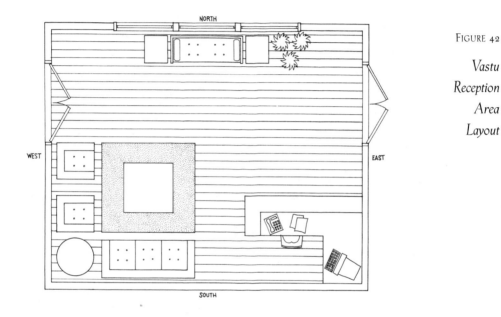

FIGURE 42

*Vastu
Reception
Area
Layout*

If you have the wherewithal to do this, hang an Indian toran over the entrance door so that everyone who comes to the company will feel welcomed and showered with invisible blessings. As always, the center of the reception area should be empty so that the spiritual power of Brahma can radiate in every direction. If the reception area is an enclosed room, the receptionist should sit in the south or west and face the northeast, the north, or the east. Facing northeast is particularly beneficial to the receptionist. The positive energies that infuse the room enter from this direction.

The zone of tranquility should, again, be a place of quiet focus or retreat. For a reception area, you might think about adding a weathered wood-slat garden bench with cushions and a collection of plants in the north or the east, close to the northeastern corner. Visitors' chairs or sofas, which are heavy, should be positioned near the west wall, the realm of Lord Varuna, or the southwest wall, the realm of Pitri, lord of ancestors.

CONFERENCE ROOM OR BOARDROOM

FIGURE 43

*Vastu
Conference
Room
Layout*

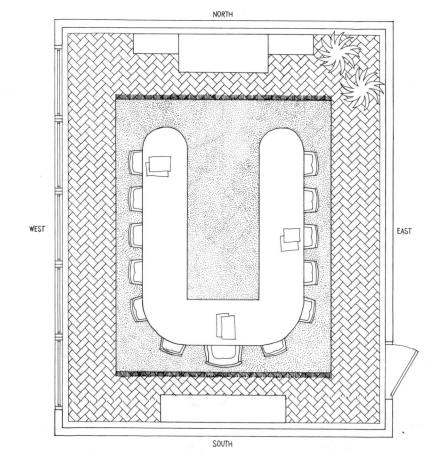

A conference room or boardroom can be located in the east or west. The east inspires inspiration and enlightenment. The west is relatively neutral and won't stifle the exchange of ideas. Because this room requires a large table that would ordinarily cover the center of the room, you might try a table with a U-shape and rounded corners. A rounded table creates dynamic energy, which is ideal in this space, where meetings frequently involve brainstorming sessions or presentations that call for an open exchange of ideas and constructive interaction. And the U-shape would leave the sacred center space free. If your company uses a circular or oval table that covers the sacred center and you find that your meetings are not effective, you should consider making a symbolic appeasement to Brahma. (See Chapter 9, *Appeasing the Gods—Appeasing Your Soul*.)

Placing a rectangular kilim on the floor that extends about two feet beyond the edge of the table introduces nature and restores harmony, with the rectangle representing becalming static energy.

The ideal place for the leader of the meeting would be in a southern chair facing north. If the leader is the chief executive of the company, the primary financial executive should sit to the CEO's right so that the financial executive also faces north, the realm of wealth. Other company employees should sit in the remaining seats in the south and along the west. They will be facing the north, the northeast, or the east—positive directions that will motivate the company employees. Visitors should sit along the eastern and northern ends of the table. Facing west, they face Varuna, the lord of oceans and the unknown; facing south, they are looking at the realm of Yama, lord of judgment and death. In this instance, the notion of dharma (duty) comes to the fore.

If you intend to show presentations, choose to screen them on the north wall, which provides health or wealth, or on the east wall, which brings enlightenment. Cover the windows with shades made out of soft natural linen. Shades can be adjusted to suit any need. A computer workstation should be placed in the southeast, which belongs to the element of fire. If the center sacred space is covered, this adds importance to the presence of a zone of tranquility, which ideally should be in the northeast, the east, or the north. A display of floor plants set in terracotta planters would be lovely.

This gathering room should feel like an organic space so that it binds everyone together and speaks of our relationship with nature. This reinforces respect and an acceptance of mutual divinity, which, in turn, creates a positive attitude and helps to subjugate individually powerful egos. The focus remains on the business welfare of the company.

CANTEEN OR CAFETERIA

The canteen or cafeteria should be located in the element of fire, which is the southeast, with the dining area toward the west or the east, in the northern half of the space. The cooking area should be in the south end of the room. Since the refrigerator is probably the heaviest item, it acts as a good barrier to retain positive energy. Place it against the south or the west wall near the southwest corner, which belongs to the earth element. Preferably, the door should open to the east. All cooking appliances that generate heat, from a cooking grill to a microwave oven or coffee maker, should be in the southeast quadrant.

The food preparation counter should be placed so that the individual who prepares food can face east. This direction is beneficial to fresh foods. The dishwasher can be placed under the counter on the eastern wall, and the sink should be near the northeastern end of the counter so that it is located in the water element.

If the dining area is a small canteen, keep the center space empty and place a small circular table in the northwest, which belongs to the element of air. The circular table will invite conversation between coworkers, and its location will prevent you from lingering too long, so that others can use the limited space. But never hurry; rushing your way through your meal is a good way to aggravate your body's constitution. The zone of tranquility in a canteen should be in the northeast quadrant. If the sun shines into the room, you can hang a basket containing *tulsi*, a form of the basil plant considered holy in many parts of the world. The sacred basil leaves nourish the soul.

If the dining area is a cafeteria, workers should eat in the east just north of the kitchen. When arranging the chairs and tables, which can be circular, square, or rectangular, keep the sacred center space empty. Vastu living emphasizes holism and sound environmental principles; you don't want to feel as if you're eating in a fast-food joint. You will sense an immediate difference in the quality of your lunchtime experience if you use organic place mats and crockery, and metal utensils, instead of Styrofoam or disposable plastic dishes and utensils. If there are bathrooms, they can be placed in any quadrant but the northeast.

Create a zone of tranquility in the north or the east with a rustic table that displays something like a big basket of dried flowers on an antique piece of lace, symbolizing nature and the cycle of time, respectively. Place a dhurrie on the floor of that zone. On the wall you could hang two wrought-iron sconces with fat low candles that flicker during mealtimes. Pipe in music that is rich in meaning, but tranquil. Of course ragas (Indian classical music) would be perfect, but other gentle sounds would also be fine; just stay away from Muzak. The dining room should have a welcoming ambience that reinforces mutual respect. The food should be nurturing and healthy, and indicative of the climate and season.

EXECUTIVE OFFICES

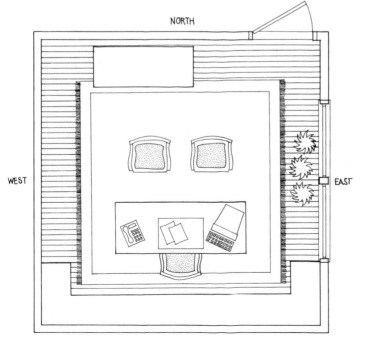

FIGURE 44

Vastu Office Layout

Room Orientation

The ideal entrance to an office is in the north or the east near the northeast corner so that the office receives the flow of the positive energy that enters the company premises from the northeast, the gateway to the gods. This energy maintains a calming influence.

Chief Executive Officer

The chief executive of the company should have an office in the southwest quadrant, the realm of the earth element and ancestors. This quadrant signifies strength and wisdom.

Managing Director

The managing director should have an office in the west, adjacent to the chief executive office. If the company has a large space, the managing director's office can also be in the southwest quadrant but on the western side of it. The managing director can then get the benefit of this area's strength and wisdom. If the company space is small, the office will still be close to this quadrant.

Chief Financial Executive

The office of the chief financial executive can be located in the north of the company. This is the realm of Kuber, the lord of wealth. The other acceptable location for the financial executive is to the right of the chief executive's office in the south. This is the appropriate choice if the two executives interact daily and make mutual decisions.

PROTECT YOUR ENERGIES

Furniture, except for cabinetry, shelves, or counters that are built into a wall, should be four inches from the wall.

Furniture Placement

Remember to keep the center space empty even if it is only two-foot square. Officials of a company as well as all the employees need to receive the spiritual power that radiates out from this sacred point of the room. It keeps us all connected to the Supreme Creator and makes us accept our divinity and respect the divinity of all existence. The desk of each executive should be in the south near the southwest so that the executive faces the north or the northeast or the east. The computer should be placed on or near the desk so that the executive faces east and is filled with inspiration when looking at the monitor.

Guests should sit opposite the executive's desk in comfortable chairs that face south. This keeps the power and leadership with the executive. The zone of tranquility should be in the north, the northeast, or the east of the office space. The zone should be personalized so that the executive, with a hundred issues on his or her mind, will be drawn to the zone in the course of a day.

If the executive requires a television set, it should be kept in the northwest quadrant, the location of the element of air and movement. In this quadrant, the television will not become a distraction. Built-in storage, counters, and cabinets should be in the south or the west where they help to retain the cosmic energies.

Special Touches

The executive should bring his soul into the office by displaying a few personal objects or wall hangings, from pictures and photographs to tapestries. Pictures of ancestors should be placed on the south or the west wall near the southwest corner. All the choices in the décor should reflect the preference of the executive, not the interests of an interior decorator. These objects bring the executive's personality into the room—the personality that helps define the inner self.

Never overlook the importance of nature. Introduce lots of plants and greenery, and use area rugs that contain the colors of nature. Have lighting that can be altered in the course of a day. If there are windows, use organic fabrics and window treatments that can be adjusted according to the sun's intensity. The presence of one's personality and of nature makes an office comfortable. They introduce a sense of well-being and reduce the formality that prevents relaxation and increases stress.

Ambience

A vastu living office reaffirms respect and appreciation of equality. Even though executives in a company have titles and power, they should, for the ultimate good of the company, strive to be approachable. An executive office, therefore, should be warm and inviting. Anyone who enters should feel comfortable in this office. If the office is formal and promotes an over-bearing attitude, conversations freeze. Talk becomes stilted and restrained. Workers feel intimidated and do not speak their mind or become too afraid to express a new idea that could benefit the company. The company loses out in the end when the environment reflects exclusion, not inclusion.

THE CUBICLE

FIGURE 45

Vastu Cubicle Layout

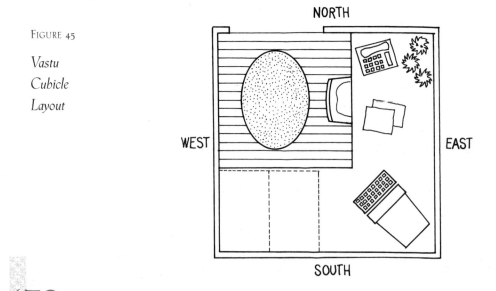

A cubicle is ordinarily quite small and filled with built-in furniture, except for the chair. In most offices, the cubicles look alike—they are sterile and dehumanizing. When you work in a cubicle that is an exact or near copy of forty other cubicles, you feel your personal identity squeezed out of the space. But small *can* become cozy. And vastu living can turn your cubicle into an extension of your self. Your personality and needs can remove the sameness—in a quiet way that does not mimic the décor of an over-energized college dorm room.

Honor the Auspicious Center Space

The typical cubicle usually has furniture lined against two or three walls so that there is, in fact, an empty center space. That's a blessing, so cherish it. Put a small attractive rug in this location so that you always remember the sacredness of the space, with its spiritual power that circulates around you. Walls can block out a lot of positive energy, which may explain why most doctors' examination rooms, which usually lack windows, feel cold and unfriendly, and it may explain why so many people hate elevators.

But most cubicles lack a door and many lack a window, so we need to break the monotony of walls and neutral color. Why not put up brackets near each corner and hang jute baskets filled with trailing silk flowers? The jute basket is organic, silkworms spun the silk for the flowers, and the flowers celebrate nature. You can also hang a collection of antique scarves on brackets. They suggest continuity and the ever-recurring cycle of life. Let your personality determine your choices, but keep the choices subdued. Your space is small and too much stuff destroys proportion.

Look around your cubicle; do you see plastic receptacles on your desk or a plastic wastebasket? Consider replacing them all with wood or clay pottery or small woven baskets to hold paper clips, pens and pencils. Find a wooden or jute wastebasket. Organic products warm up a space, especially one that is dominated by a utilitarian décor. Do you work on a computer? Keep it in the southeast and position the monitor so that you face the east, the direction of enlightenment, or the north, the direction of health and wealth, or the northeast, the gateway to the gods.

When you create a zone of tranquility, be sure that it embraces you and your connection to nature. Given the size of the cubicle, why not place the zone within reach? The best locations would be on your desk or counter in the east, the northeast, or the north. You could place a picture of someone or something that you love next to an old wooden box or a shallow clay bowl filled with dried flower petals or sea glass or just sand—anything that is natural and pleasing to the touch. In the course of a day, focus for a few minutes on your personal display until your mind is emptied of thoughts and you are reenergized.

Follow these vastu living guidelines and you will break up the sameness and monotony that so often defines the cubicle. You will create a space that is organic and personal. The ambience will boost your spirits, connect to your soul, and reduce your stress.

THE OPEN SPACE

The open space obviously lacks privacy. Unless you are situated near a wall, your space also lacks any visible boundaries and feels undefined. All this is true, but vastu living can still be brought into the part of the open space that contains you and your aura. The lack of walls can also be viewed as an asset. Fewer walls mean that the positive energies that enter the company from the northeast quadrant are free to move through the open space. They are not blocked, so you become the recipient of lots of positive energy.

To draw your personality into an open space is a challenge. You probably don't want to be garishly eccentric and not fit in with your "neighborhood." But you can still quietly personalize your space and introduce that necessary connection with nature. First, define your space on the vastu purusha mandala. Draw a quadrangle that extends beyond your desk and chair by one or two feet depending on the size of the empty area, if there is any, between you and the neighboring desks. Call this quadrangle your work area and make it your own space. Fence it in. If your work area receives good sun light, put a plant near your desk (but not where people will trip over it) or on your desk so that everyone is constantly reminded of the beauty and importance of nature.

Honor the Auspicious Center Space

Unfortunately, within the "boundaries" of your own work area, the desk or chair will normally cover the sacred center. Place a small oval rug or rattan mat under your chair and under part of the desk to mark the center where the spiritual power should be free to circulate. Make a symbolic appeasement to Brahma and the element of space (see Chapter 9, *Appeasing the Gods—Appeasing Your Soul*). Follow the guidelines described in The Cubicle, above, to create a zone of tranquility. Consider incorporating your appeasement into this zone.

Sit facing the north, the northeast, or the east. This may mean that you need to try to turn the desk around, which might be impossible if you are sitting in clusters, desk to desk. But if you can turn your desk so that you face one of these directions, do it. These directions are important for inner peace. If possible, place your computer on the southeastern side of your desk, and then put an attractive cushion covered with a natural fabric or an old piece of fabric against the back of your chair to increase your comfort and add color to the space. Finally, of course, become friendly with your neighbors. We are all interconnected and divine.

If nothing feels quite right after these attempts (and remember, a benchmark of fifty percent success with vastu is fine enough), try talking with your superiors or colleagues about switching desks with someone else. This is not an impossible request, and might begin a movement to help improve the atmosphere of the whole office.

W HEN YOU INCORPORATE vastu living into your personal workspace, you will have an ambience that welcomes you as soon as you step inside. The space is warm and familiar because it represents you and your divinity. Positive energy circulates so that you are energized and can focus on your work. You will increase your sense of satisfaction if you: 1) accept the belief that it is important to work slowly, 2) enjoy each stage of the process, and 3) find comfort in the work that you are doing now.

Giving yourself permission to take breaks to empty your mind calms you and leaves you reinvigorated. The acknowledgment of nature keeps you connected to the outside world. Your soul becomes aware of everything that pulsates along with you. The harmony and positive energy that come with a vastu living workspace reduce the stress that is far too often a huge part of your work life.

❀ 8 ❀

THE GIFT OF NATURE

The hymn—"Take Thou a Lesson from the Tree" is worth laying to one's heart. The tree bears the heat of the sun and yet provides cool shade to us. What do we do?

—MAHATMA GANDHI

LOOK AT A weeping willow and watch its gentle leaves brush against the earth. Smell the fragrance of a rose, frangipani, holy basil, or rosemary. Draw in the odor of the earth after a rainfall, or even while you water your indoor plants. Walk through a grove and hear the crunch of leaves under your feet and enjoy the sweet smell of pine. Stare into the darkness at that perfect time when you experience the joy of daybreak with its inspiring burst of color. Most of us pause to absorb these moments and even find ourselves thinking about the amazing force that created all this wonder. Some of us think of these moments as "communing with nature."

We must never forget the foundation behind vastu, the Vedic wisdom that gives our practice of vastu its spiritual dimension. Vastu wants us to celebrate nature, specifically our link to nature. Nothing is random in the universe, and we must honor and revere all that shares our world. Every thing, including all of nature's gifts and each one of us, are connected to the Supreme Creative Force that we feel when we experience nature's splendor. Nature surrounds us with peace and makes the soul feel good because it brings us closer to the ultimate goal: the discovery of the Truth. Tat Tvam Asi—"Thou Art That."

With vastu living, we also honor nature because, like us, it is an expression of the five basic elements: space, air, fire, water, and earth. Fire, in this instance, doesn't refer to wild fires that consume precious woodlands. The element of fire in plants is life-giving. Nature absorbs sunlight, and sunlight creates sap in plants. Sunlight induces the cycle of life—growth, preservation, and finally decomposition. Without the harmonious presence of the five elements in our home or our workplace, we can never establish a lasting harmony for ourselves. This is true about the property around our home and workplace. The proper use of nature in our environments can increase our feeling of comfort.

LANDSCAPES AND OUTDOOR GARDENS

PREPARATION OF YOUR SITE

If you are clearing your property, save any boulders or stones that you find. The larger rocks are useful in a rock garden and smaller ones can be part of a border along a walkway. Please, don't clear trees indiscriminately. Also consider leaving tree stumps just where they are. You can turn them into a seat or a place to put a plant or even a birdbath.

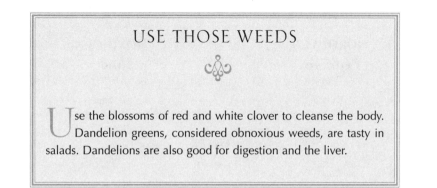

USE THOSE WEEDS

Use the blossoms of red and white clover to cleanse the body. Dandelion greens, considered obnoxious weeds, are tasty in salads. Dandelions are also good for digestion and the liver.

All these guidelines not only show respect for nature, but also decrease the level of disturbance to the energies that originally flowed through the existing environment. If you build a fence around your property, use a wood or stone fence and cover it with vines. Fences are wonderful screens, but by using natural products and plants, you emphasize decoration and the beauty of nature and not exclusivity or isolation.

HONOR THE ELEMENTS

When you are ready to introduce nature into the interior of your home or your workplace, or to add plants to your property, first work out your plans with a compass and draw them onto a copy, or copies, of the vastu purusha mandala. Try not to disturb the harmonious relationship of the elements. But since your climate can dictate the placement of trees and plants on your property, remember that you can always make an appeasement if you upset the harmony of the elements and their deities. The symbolic appeasement can also add an unexpected and attractive dimension to an outdoor setting. See Chapter 9, *Appeasing the Gods—Appeasing Your Soul.*

INTERMEDIATE DIRECTIONS

NORTHWEST

ELEMENT:
Air

DEITY:
Vayu

NORTHEAST

ELEMENT:
Water

DEITY:
Isa

CENTER

ELEMENT:
Space

DEITY:
Brahma

SOUTHWEST

ELEMENT:
Earth

DEITY:
Pitri

SOUTHEAST

ELEMENT:
Fire

DEITY:
Agni

Northeast—Water

- Ideally, a pool or pond or any water source belongs in the northeast quadrant, which belongs to the element of water and is the gateway to the gods. Water in this quadrant acts as a beneficial receptacle for the positive energy that comes from the northeast.
- Medicinal plants, such as violets and clustered dandelions (yes, dandelions), are an attractive ground cover (honest, even the dandelions) or a perfect border for the pond or the walk area surrounding a pool. Introduce water plants, such as medicinal water lilies.
- Height and density block the positive energy that flows into the property from the northeast and the sunrise, so avoid tall trees in this quadrant. Consider putting a small tree with colorful blooms, such as a dogwood, near the eastern border of the pond or pool. Its reflection in the pool is lovely and inspires positive thoughts that are a reminder of the importance of this quadrant and also of the east, the realm of Surya, the sun god and sustainer of life.

- Water wells should be in the northeast quadrant. But obviously, if you need a well and the best water source is located in another quadrant, or you have a well already in place in a different quadrant that supplies good water, don't even consider closing it up. But do make an appeasement (see Chapter 9, *Appeasing the Gods—Appeasing Your Soul*).

Southeast—Fire

- The southeast, the realm of the element of fire, is a good area for herbs, edible flowers, berries, and vegetables that thrive in the sun. If your kitchen is in the southeast, you can step outside your kitchen door and have the freshest ingredients at your fingertips.
- If some of the vegetables and spices need shade, plant edible sunflowers, which are the color of fire. They will act as an umbrella for shade-loving plants.

Southwest—Earth

- Honor the element of earth by building up a mound in the southwest quadrant for a rock garden. Be creative with the garden and include decomposing tree trunks that have been felled and would otherwise be removed. Train low-lying vines to grow over the trunks. Grow pansies, violets, or lilies-of-the-valley in front of the vines. Include stones, statues, miniature evergreen shrubs and plants that bloom in the winter, such as winter jasmine, and lots of wildflowers. You want to establish a little world here that reveals the diversity in nature.
- Place tall trees in this quadrant. They will block out the heat that collects here. If you create a rock garden, put the trees behind the garden or to its west or to the extreme southeast so that the leaves don't block out all the sun. The objective is to create height and density to trap the positive energies and keep them inside your property.

Northwest—Air

- The northwest is the realm of the element of air. For privacy in this quadrant, add a hedge of beech that you prune so that it is low and dense. You can also use an unpruned hedge of yew, which spreads out and assumes its naturally appealing shape.
- Put a leafy tree, such as a maple, in this quadrant, where the shimmering leaves move with the air and also honor the cycle of life with their seasonal changes.
- Surround the base of any tree with flowers that bloom before the onset of new leaves, such as tulips, crocus, narcissus. Blend in a flowering ground cover, such as violets and lilies-of-the-valley, which do well in the shade that comes with the thick new maple leaves.

Sacred Center—Space

It may be impossible to keep the center of a property empty. The plot may be too small. So honor the element of space and the region of Brahma with a container of holy basil at the foot of your home or your workspace. Or put a welcoming sign, such as AUM, on the front entrance door. This is the primordial word that set creation in motion. For other appeasements, refer to Chapter 9, *Appease the Gods—Appease Your Soul*.

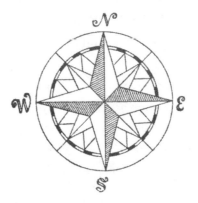

REMEMBER THE CARDINAL DIRECTIONS

NORTH

DEITY:
Soma and Kuber

IDENTIFICATION:
Health and Wealth

WEST

DEITY:
Varuma

IDENTIFICATION:
Unknown and Darkness

EAST

DEITY:
Surya

IDENTIFICATION:
Enlightenment and Inspiration

SOUTH

DEITY:
Yama

IDENTIFICATION:
Death, Duty, and Responsibility

North

- The north, which is the realm of Soma, the lord of health, is a wonderful place to grow medicinal plants and fragrant plants or shrubs where just the scent can make you feel good. Good choices include holy basil, flowering chamomile (roman chamomile makes a wonderful ground cover), coriander (coriander can thrive in partial shade), lavender (lavender repels moths), marigolds (butterflies love marigolds), roses, snapdragons, lilacs, and honeysuckle.
- Shrubs and hedges along the northern edge of the property or near the home add privacy. Select seasonal flowering plants and evergreens to suggest the cycle of life.

East

- Honor Surya, the sun god who rules over the east. If you have good sun, plant colorful flowers. Create a garden with plants that ascend to the center on either side to bless this deity who brings us enlightenment.

- Near the eastern edge of the property, create a hedge of berries or flowering shrubs. If you want complete privacy from an adjacent property, put up a fence and grow flowering vines that also include edible climbers, such as cucumbers. At the base of the fence, plant strawberries.
- Reject trees that block the sunrise.

South

- Plants in the south, which belongs to Yama, the lord of death, should also serve to prevent the escape of the beneficial energies that travel in an arc from the northeast. Plant tall trees or a dense hedge using bushes and shrubs that suit the climate in your area.
- Build a stone wall, fence, or trellis and cover it with vines—some that flower, such as clematis, honeysuckle, hydrangea, morning glory (hummingbirds love morning glory), and wisteria; and some that are evergreen (ivy) or bloom in the winter (winter jasmine).

West

- Tall trees on your property should also be in the west to help retain the positive energy. In many climates, trees in the west can also help block the wind.
- For privacy, establish a dense hedge with shrubbery that suits your climate, or erect a fence and cover it with shade-loving creeper and climbers, such as evergreen ivy and pachysandra and winter jasmine

ZONE OF TRANQUILITY

A zone of tranquility in the garden gives us an opportunity to incorporate personally meaningful objects on our property so that being outdoors is comfortable and beckoning. Creating a meditative zone in the north, the northeast, or the east gives you a place to sit in quiet and reenergize or just concentrate on the sounds, smells, and scents of nature until your mind emp-ties and thoughts turn inward.

If you have a large property, create a couple of zones. Divide the proper-ty into quadrants and locate a zone in the north, the northeast, or the east of each quadrant. Consider hanging a hammock or a garden swing there, putting out a bench, or making a cozy seating arrangement. These appeal-ing environments will encourage you to be outside to enjoy the fresh air and the good feelings that come with nature.

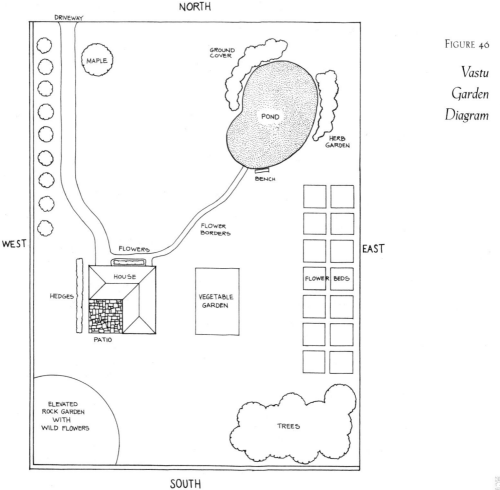

FIGURE 46

Vastu Garden Diagram

CELEBRATING NATURE INDOORS

If your home or workplace lacks sunlight, you can still include the presence of nature. Try displaying bouquets, flower petals floating in bowls of water, or dried flowers. Or hang a string of garlic bulbs or red chilies.

Nature can also be acknowledged through the display of a collection of stones, seashells, pinecones, acorns, shelled nuts, baskets, or boxes made of woven grass or reed. You can even honor nature with symbols: paintings and etchings that use earthy tones; floor and window treatments, waste baskets, and storage receptacles made of organic materials; stone, metal, or wood statues.

But if you do have a home or workspace that provides sunlight, try to celebrate the sun with plants. Think about creating a special area where the plants are arranged according to height with the tallest in the middle. This recreates an ascent, mirroring the temple, and is extremely pleasing to the eye and the soul.

If you have a terrace, balcony, porch, or verandah, why not create a mini-outdoor environment? You can choose plants and trees that thrive in the direction of the attached outdoor space. Use containers, hanging baskets, and window boxes. But please keep the proportion of the space in mind and don't overwhelm it. Also, be sure to include a zone of tranquility and try to put it in the east, the north, or the northeast. Within the zone, create an inviting space that beckons you to sit or even lie down to enjoy the outdoors.

SACRED BASIL

Indian homes traditionally place a pot containing *tulsi*, a plant sacred to Vishnu, the Hindu god of preservation, in the courtyard if one exists or just outside the home. Tulsi is holy basil and the plant is worthy of its name. It is extremely fragrant, tasty, and leads to spiritual growth.

HONOR THE ELEMENTS

Inside your home or workplace, honor each element with its corresponding deity through the use of plants or flowers, organic objects, or a symbolic representation of nature that is connected to each specific element or deity. You can honor the element in its quadrant within the home or workplace or within each room.

INTERMEDIATE DIRECTIONS

NORTHWEST

ELEMENT:
Air

DEITY:
Vayu

NORTHEAST

ELEMENT:
Water

DEITY:
Isa

CENTER

ELEMENT:
Space

DEITY:
Brahma

SOUTHWEST

ELEMENT:
Earth

DEITY:
Pitri

SOUTHEAST

ELEMENT:
Fire

DEITY:
Agni

187

Northeast—Water

- The northeast quadrant of your home or workplace or individual rooms belongs to the element of water and is the gateway to the gods. If there is a window with good sun, keep a terracotta pot filled with holy basil, the sacred plant that is associated with spiritual growth in India. Complement the holy basil with a window box containing yellow nasturtium and blue pansies (the colors of peace and meditation).
- If the kitchen is in the northeast and has a sunny window, grow an indoor herbal garden that includes holy basil. The northeast is the element of water, and each time you water these plants, you will be honoring the element of this quadrant.
- If you lack a window or sunlight in this quadrant, put out a vase of flowers or a bowl of water filled with petals. This will bless the element and its deity.

Southeast—Fire

- The southeast quadrant in your home or workplace or in an individual room belongs to the element of fire. Fire is manifested in the sun, which sustains all life and helps plants thrive.
- If the kitchen is in the southeast and receives good sun, this is an appropriate location for an herbal garden on shelves in the window, and vegetables, such as cherry tomatoes, that hang from a basket. Put edible nasturtiums and violets or just strawberries in a window box. Place a small aloe plant on the kitchen counter so that you can break off a piece and use its therapeutic powers in case you burn or cut yourself while cooking.
- If you lack a window or sunlight in the southeast, place a lamp with an organic base in this quadrant and keep the lamp lit to honor fire.

Southwest—Earth

- The southwestern quadrant in your home, workspace, or individual room is a good place for dense ferns or potted trees on the floor if windows provide enough sun. These plants help hold in the positive

188

energies that flow in from the northeast quadrant. The soil and the pot, which should be made of clay, celebrate the earth element.

- If you lack a window or sunlight, display an organic object that is created from clay.

Northwest—Air

- The northwest belongs to the element of air. Place plants here that are leafy and rustle if there is a breeze from an open window or fan. Consider ferns and trailing plants that hang from containers.
- If you don't have a window or environment for plants that need care, consider getting dried flowers that are feathery.

Sacred Center—Space

The center of any interior area belongs to the element of space and Brahma. The center should be left empty so that spiritual power flows in every direction. An appropriate way to honor this element through the presence of nature is to place natural tiles or an area rug made of natural fiber—silk, cotton, wool, camelhair—or a jute or grass mat in one of the center spaces in the home or workspace.

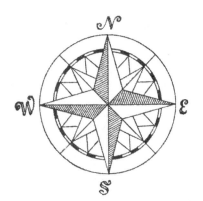

189

Remember the Cardinal Directions

NORTH

DEITY:
Soma and Kuber

IDENTIFICATION:
Health and Wealth

WEST

DEITY:
Varuma

IDENTIFICATION:
Unknown and Darkness

EAST

DEITY:
Surya

IDENTIFICATION:
Enlightenment and Inspiration

SOUTH

DEITY:
Yama

IDENTIFICATION:
Death, Duty, and Responsibility

North

- The north belongs to Soma, the lord of health. If the north of your interior space has windows with some sun, grow medicinal plants and fragrant plants. Consider pansies, ginger, red pepper. Select seasonal flowering plants to suggest the cycle of life.

East

- Surya, the sun god, rules over the east. If you have windows in the east that provide good sun, choose colorful flowering plants and grow an herbal or vegetable garden in a window box or on shelves.
- Start a small indoor garden where the plants growing on either side ascend to the center. The display is beautiful and honors the god and enlightenment.

South

- The south honors Yama, the lord of both death and dharma (duty). Since vastu suggests placing load-bearing objects in the south, you

FIGURE 47

*Vastu
Terrace
Garden*

can bless Yama with heavier plants, such as indoor palm or rubber plants or an umbrella tree.

West

- The west belongs to Varuna, the lord of darkness or the unknown. If you have a window, the sill is an ideal place for shade-loving plants. They will thrive in the limited light from the west.
- If you have no natural light source along the west wall of the workplace or apartment, then just treat this quadrant to an occasional bouquet of flowers, or incorporate a couple of organic products in this direction that ushers in the night.

Once you bring an abundance of nature into your home and workspace, you will love how it enriches your décor and you will appreciate how it calms your soul. We are connected to nature. When it is not present in our home or workspace, we lose sight of this vital link. Nature also expresses, through its beauty, the order and harmony that prevails in the universe. By honoring nature inside our home and workspace, we also honor the perfection of divine creation.

 **9**

APPEASING THE GODS—
APPEASING YOUR SOUL

A fault, as small as a mustard seed, becomes as big as a mountain when sought to be concealed. It can, however, be eradicated if an open confession is made.

—MAHATMA GANDHI

WHEN WE BRING vastu living into our homes, workspaces, or properties, we invariably face problems involving the improper placement of the elements that we are unable to correct. You may have a bathroom located in the northeast or a kitchen stuck in the southwest. In the course of reading this book, you have frequently been directed to this chapter to learn about the symbolic appeasements you can make to the so-called offended elements and their respective deities to solve these vastu living problems. The solutions fall into two categories: the reestablishment of harmony through the use of color, and the reestablishment of harmony through the appeasement of a metaphorical deity. You can

choose whichever solution you prefer. They each add strength to your surroundings. They each work as appeasements to the offended element or elements and restore harmony, including the harmony of your own soul.

EXAMPLES OF COMMON PROBLEMS

- Your kitchen is in the southwest quadrant when it should be in the
  southeast. To be certain that you have not offended the element of
  the southwest, earth, and the element of the southeast, fire, you
  should play it safe and make an appeasement to keep the harmony
  in balance.
- Your bathroom is in the northeast quadrant of your apartment.
  Worse, the toilet is in the northeastern quadrant of the bathroom.
  The northeast is the element of water, but unfortunately it is also the
  gateway to the gods and must never be contaminated by bathroom
  waste. You'll want to make an appeasement to the element of water.
- You have a fabulous swimming pool, the joy of the household. But
  swimming pools belong in the northeast, the realm of the element
  of water, and yours is located in the southwest so that your family
  can enjoy the hot southern sun. Though you have no intention of
  moving the pool, according to the vastu guidelines, the southwest,
  which belongs to the element of earth, should serve as a barrier to
  hold in the positive energy that flows through the property. You'll
  want to protect yourself and make an appeasement to each of the
  offended elements—earth and water.
- You work in an open area with about twelve other people. Your personal space is not much larger than your desk, and so you have no
  way to respect the sanctity of Brahma's realm, which is in the direct
  center of your small area. If fact, when you sit at your desk, Brahma's
  realm, which belongs to the element of space, is right under your
  feet. To keep the spiritual power flowing in your tiny work area, you
  should make an appeasement to the element of space.

- Your favorite tree is an old oak that stands tall in the northeast quadrant of your property. The oak was one of the reasons you bought the house. It's lovely height and thick branches, however, mean it obstructs the flow of the positive energy that enters this quadrant, which belongs to the element of water and is the gateway to the gods. Tall trees should be located in the southwest quadrant of the property. You should keep the elements of water and earth happy by making an appeasement to them so that you will be happy, too.

- You have a one-bedroom apartment and the bedroom is in the southeast, which belongs to the element of fire. You also have a pitta (fire)-dominated constitution. Because of the ayurveda rule—like increases like—the quadrant of fire can create an excess of fire in your constitution. To make certain your sleep time brings you benefits and not problems, protect yourself by making an appeasement to the fire element and the element of water (which calms a fiery constitution and is the best location for your bedroom). Then harmony will prevail.

THE SOLUTIONS

THE OBJECTIVE

As you've seen, there are two different types of problems at work here: in one case, you have offended just a single element, such as the problem of the violated sacred center, and need to appease just that element and deity. Most problems, however, involve two elements, the one that has been moved to a different quadrant, and the one belonging to that different quadrant, which must also be placated since its realm has been trespassed. The harmony between these two elements and their respective deities has been disturbed. The kitchen problem is a clear example. The kitchen should be in the southeast (the element of fire), but it is in the southwest (the element of earth). This means that both elements—fire and earth—have to be appeased. Fortunately, one appeasement serves them both. You'll just want to consider the characteristics of the deities connected to each element and use something that is equally beneficial.

These same guidelines should be followed for the inappropriate placement of any element on your property or in any room. You may be shuddering, imagining your home or workspace turned into a shrine. But you will see that you have a lot of freedom in choosing appeasements that appeal to you. All your appeasements could relate to nature, for instance, or to choice of colors. Read on . . .

HARMONY IN COLOR

Long ago, Hindu sages understood the power of color and its effect on our spiritual well-being. Specific colors were often identified with a deity. The body of Brahma, for example, is normally red. Vishnu is blue. Hindu pujas incorporate red, saffron (orange), yellow, green, and white into the rituals. Red is the color of the *tikka* mark placed on the forehead. Saffron is the color of fire in the sacred altar. Yellow is a popular color of garlands that are presented to the deities. Green is represented in the sacred basil leaves that should float in the holy water. White is the color of ash—the purified residual of the sacred fire—and blue always indicates infinity and eternity. (See Color Chart below.)

Researchers in the field of geobiology have discovered that each color vibrates at its own wavelength and has a different effect on us. They have also discovered that a color that exudes certain qualities in the daytime often has a complementary color that mirrors the quality of the daytime color at night.[24]

This is why you need to place both the daytime and complementary nighttime color in the location of the offended element and deity. But you

[24] See *Studies in Geobiology*, annual research reports from 1989-1994, published by Sri Aurobindo Institute of Applied Scientific Research, Prabhat Poddar, Director of Geobiology Research. Address: Academy House, 34, Maravadi St., Padmini Nagar, Pondicherry, 605012, India.

can display these colors any way that you choose, from incorporating them into the fabric on a cushion, to draping a strip of each color across the sides of a small table, to affixing small color patches discreetly near the base of the wall.

When you choose a daytime color to appease the offended element or elements, you want to make the choice on the basis of the characteristics of the daytime color. For example, if you have offended the element of space, which belongs to Brahma, a good daytime color choice would be red, because red represents spiritual power. If you need to placate the elements of fire *and* water, a good choice would be blue. The characteristics of blue—stability, serenity, infinity—apply to the characteristics of both elements. And remember to put the colors in the location that belongs to the trespassed element or deity. For example, to pacify the elements offended by a kitchen placed in the southwest, you would put the colors in the southwest, the wrong quadrant, not in the southeast, the correct quadrant.

COLOR CHART [25]

Day Color	Color Characteristics	Night Color
Red	Represents spiritual power and has the ability to ward away evil. Red is also auspicious, can endow us with power, bravery, protection, and can induce a sense of charity.	Violet
Saffron	Represents the sacred fire and purity, and the quest for enlightenment and truth.	Indigo
White	Represents purity, peace, knowledge, and nobility.	White
Green	Represents harmony and tranquility. Identified with nature, green is soothing and therapeutic.	Green
Blue	Represents stability, serenity, and infinity. Symbolizes the cool side of nature; blue can defuse powerful emotions and improve judgment. Blue can calm down fire.	Yellow
Yellow	Represents knowledge and clarity. Yellow stimulates the mind, which leads to awareness and self-confidence.	Blue

[25]The nighttime colors are from research published in the "Studies in Geobiology: Colours-Man-Building Interrelationships" in *Annual Report 1991-92*, which is part of the collected reports by Sri Aurobindo Institute of Applied Scientific Research, mentioned above. The daytime colors are related to Hinduism.

BLESSINGS FROM THE GODS

You can also solve a problem by introducing an image of a deity or a symbolic representation of a deity. For example, you could appease the element of fire and its deity, Agni, with an image of Ganesha, the elephant-headed god and remover of obstacles. As with the use of colors, you would also place the deity or its symbol in the quadrant belonging to the element that has been trespassed. Again, taking the example of the kitchen wrongfully placed in the southwest, Ganesha would be placed in the southwest to appease the element of earth, whose realm has been trespassed, and the element of fire that has been introduced, by way of the kitchen, into the wrong quadrant. Ganesha appeases both elements.

And how did I come to use Ganesha? Ganesha's symbols have been a guiding light in my life. But you can make an appeasement with any Hindu deity, if you choose to use a Hindu deity. They are all benevolent. Just pick one whose attributes appeal to you (see the descriptions, below). Place the deity in the appropriate quadrant so that it can calm the offended elements. Let it shower them with blessings. The deity will restore the harmony in the space and the harmony within you.

The application of vastu is universal and not restricted to Hindus, but since this science originated in the Vedic way of life, here are descriptions of some of the popular Hindu deities that are revered today. You will notice that, with the exception of Brahma, the Vedic deities associated with the elements and cardinal directions are not included. As explained in Chapter 3, *Vastu in Ancient Temple and Design*, the Vedic deities slid into the background during the evolution of Hinduism. They were overshadowed by deities that remain popular today.

Brahma

Brahma is the source of knowledge and the lord of creation in the Hindu Trinity. There are many myths about the birth of Brahma. He was born from a golden egg after lying inside it for one thousand years. When Brahma finally burst out of the egg, he entered into an extended period of meditation in which he created the rest of the world. Another myth says that Brahma was born from a lotus (a symbol of purity and sacred wisdom) that grew out of the navel of Vishnu. Sitting on the lotus, which was still attached to the navel, Brahma once again sat in extended meditation. The two myths are related in terms of symbolism. The navel, as stated earlier, is the life-giving source. The egg also gave shape and life to Brahma.

FIGURE 48

Brahma

Many myths, which show the rivalry between Shiva and Brahma, offer different reasons why Shiva decided to remove one of Brahma's original five heads. One story involves incest. (Hinduism does not shy away from sexuality and its importance in ensuring the survival of mankind.) But in this myth, Brahma, who had a bit too much to drink, committed incest with his daughter. There are many versions of this story, but they all lead to the loss of a fifth head so that Brahma could no longer see in every direction and his daughter could escape. This improper behavior, it is said, explains Brahma's loss in stature and why few temples are built in his honor. But Hindu artists do show the image of Brahma in prints and in paintings of the Trinity. And sculptures of Brahma are found inside temples dedicated to other deities.

Brahma, with his four bearded heads, can still see in all the cardinal directions. Symbolically, each of his four faces represents a different *Veda*, the source of spiritual wisdom and Truth. Since this knowledge is for everyone and for all times, many assert that the four heads also stand for the four *yugas* (divisions of time allocated to the lifespan of the universe).

When Brahma is depicted with four hands, each hand represents a cardinal direction and signifies omnipotence. And whether he is shown with two or four hands, the objects held in each hand are symbolic. Brahma may carry a rosary in an upper hand. He is counting the individual beads that convey the presence of time that controls the cycle of creation, preservation, and destruction. One hand frequently holds a vessel of water to remind us that the universe evolved out of water, or a hand holds a book to remind us of the importance of knowledge. One hand could also be held in a gesture that offers protection to anyone who is determined to discover self-realization.

Brahma's eyes are the sun and the moon, his nose the cosmic *prana*, or life-sustaining breath that comes with birth. His beard is white to symbolize that the act of creation began countless years ago. His body is red to suggest birth; his robes are off-white to signify both purity and impurity—the dualities that exist. Brahma is often shown sitting or standing on either a red or white lotus, a beautiful symbol of the Eternal Truth. When the lotus is red, it speaks of activities that are involved in creation. When the lotus is white, it speaks of purity.

Brahma may be accompanied by a swan, which is called his vehicle and symbolizes knowledge and Brahma's ability to discriminate in the act of creation. The swan, also a symbol of beauty, is white, which echoes again the theme of purity. Brahma's consort is Saraswati, the goddess of wisdom and knowledge.

Saraswati

Saraswati, the consort of Brahma, is the goddess of wisdom and knowledge and the goddess of all the fine arts. Brahma requires her knowledge in the act of perfect creation. One needs knowledge to master all endeavors, especially in the fine arts. Saraswati is also the embodiment of spiritual wisdom and many Hindus refer to her as the Mother of the *Vedas*.

This goddess is normally shown with four hands. Two hands are playing the *vina* (stringed instrument) through which she makes music—the vibration of sound—and spreads the Word. She holds one of the *Vedas* to remind us of the wisdom that is contained within these texts, including the *Upanisads*. Her fourth hand holds rosaries that exemplify the need to concentrate through meditation and chanting. It is through acquired knowledge and these acts of devotion that one comes to the Truth.

Saraswati often sits on a sacred lotus or flies on the back of a peacock or a swan, which are her vehicles. Every color exists in the peacock; therefore, it represents the earthly world of objects. Sitting astride the peacock, Saraswati is above this world and in the realm of Truth. The swan, which is also Brahma's vehicle, floats on the surface of the water and echoes this same symbol. The swan reminds us that while we live in the world, we must be able to pull free of attachments and desires.

FIGURE 49

Saraswati

Shiva

Shiva is conceivably the most popular deity in the Hindu Trinity. One reason behind his popularity is the Hindu belief that this Lord of Destruction destroys the impediments that prevent the soul from discovering its connection to the Supreme Creative Force. Secondly, given the ongoing cycle of life and death, Hindus realize that destruction must occur before creation can begin again. So Shiva is considered a benevolent re-creator who is always encouraging us to do better. Considered the supreme deity in the Vedic Era, Shiva is also called the Mahadeva or

FIGURE 50

Shiva

Great God. His creative powers have led to the worship of the Shiva Linga (phallus), which is frequently found inside a temple's inner sanctum. It is so potent that the linga is the only symbol of a deity that can be placed in the exact center of the sanctum.

This powerful god is also a meditative deity. Often depicted with his eyes half closed, Shiva's thoughts are drawn inward, which reminds us that this is the path to self-realization. This deity, who is also the Lord of Yoga, is perceived as an ascetic: meditative and spiritually powerful. When he fights evil, his actions remind us to destroy needless thoughts, distractions, and attachments, which prevent our own spiritual growth.

Shiva's three eyes also speak of his power. The eyes on the left and right represent the sun and the moon; in other words, the outer world. The third eye in the middle of the forehead represents destruction. Some say that the third eye also represents fire. Because fire is the source of knowledge and enlightenment, the third eye also symbolizes the ultimate truth of the inner self and reaffirms Shiva's position as the Lord of Yoga.

Shiva is frequently depicted with a blue throat. Once, he willingly swallowed poison during a battle with demons over the gift of the nectar of immortality. He holds the poison in his neck, which turned it blue. Shiva's matted hair carries the sacred River Ganga. The ornament of the crescent moon in his hair carries the precious nectar. The poison and the nectar symbolize the dualities in our existence and remind us that we must accept them all and not let them affect us. The crescent moon is also a symbol of time. The moon with its cycle of waxing and waning is the governing principle of the universe.

The rest of Shiva's body is fair-colored, symbolic of peace. It is also strewn with ashes. The ashes remind us that everything eventually decomposes to ashes or dust. This is yet another reminder to follow Shiva's example so that we will find salvation. Shiva normally has a cobra comfortably draped around his body. Cobras are poisonous and represent negative attributes, such as anger and jealousy. The cobra's presence accentuates Shiva's power.

Shiva, who can go beyond the material world of objects, renders the cobra harmless. Other aspects of the cobra relate to Shiva. Cobras rarely create their own home; they usually borrow homes made by other creatures. They also live a long time without nourishment, and they inhabit remote places. Shiva lives on the remote crest of Mount Kailash in the Himalayas, where he spends long periods of time in uninterrupted meditation. In sum, the cobra's behavior stands as a symbol of the perfect yogi, who shows restraint and renunciation.

Everything about Shiva is connected to the path to salvation. It is even common to see one of his hands forming the *chinmudra*, in which the index finger is bent down to the thumb to create a zero. This mudra reminds each of us to bend our ego—reduce it to a zero—and destroy its false importance. Shiva's vehicle is Nandi, the devoted bull and symbol of spiritual strength and the power of wisdom in action. Shiva's consort is the goddess Parvati who assumes many forms, including Durga.

Parvati and Durga

Parvati

Parvati, the consort of Shiva, is the golden-colored goddess of power and strength. She represents the *Shakti* (female power or active energy) of Shiva and is considered a mother goddess who assumes many forms that complement each form of Shiva. As Parvati, she embodies goodness and is considered the ideal woman. Her emergence out of the ocean of milk makes her a symbol of utmost purity. Adorned in splendor, Parvati is often shown with all her manifestations, such as Durga.

FIGURE 51

Parvati

Durga

Durga is the wrathful protector and a symbol of power. Durga overcomes the evil and demons that reside within us. With a weapon in each of her eight hands, she is ready to destroy any weakness that keeps us from the Truth. Each weapon, a gift from a deity, exists as a symbol of an appropriate quality that can lead to success: determination, concentration, clarity of thought, strength, energy. Durga usually rides a lion or tiger, which only attacks when it is threatened or hungry. But when the animal does attack, it is ferocious and hard to restrain. These animals are the ego, and Durga's subjugation of either the lion or tiger symbolizes the subjugation of the ego.

FIGURE 52

Durga

205

FIGURE 53

Ganesha

Ganesha

Ganesha, the elephant-headed god, is the first deity worshipped in Hindu ceremonies. The benevolent elephant, with his potbelly and his preference for sweets, is the remover of obstacles and the god of auspicious new beginnings. But Ganesha did not begin life with an elephant's head. Hindu legend claims that while Shiva was away from his wife Parvati, she created a son out of the oil rubbed on her body. When Shiva returned, this unknown son prevented Shiva from seeing Parvati. Shiva chopped off the boy's head. Parvati was so distraught that Shiva promised to restore life to his son with the head of the first creature he encountered. It was an elephant.

Ganesha's appearance is symbolically potent, representing wisdom and discretion. The wide ears allow Ganesha to listen continuously and allow him to receive abundant spiritual knowledge, which his large head can easily disseminate and retain. His trunk, which can rip out a tree or pick up a needle, is sensitive enough to be gentle. The trunk can also be powerful enough to remove any obstacle that hinders an individual seeking the knowledge that leads to enlightenment, or to put obstacles in the path of an individual who shuns this path. His mouth and stomach are large so that he can eat enormous amounts of food, which symbolize all the experiences, good and bad, that come with life.

The rat is the surprising vehicle of Ganesha. While a rat is normally a nuisance, this rat is obedient. It sits near food but doesn't take it. It has mastered the urge and honors the commands of Ganesha. The rat is symbolic of our own desires, which we must subjugate to reach our spiritual goal.

Vishnu

Vishnu, the preserver and third deity in the Hindu Trinity, is also popular. As the preserver of the universe, Vishnu is filled with mercy and devotion for all creation. Vishnu often appears with a serpent with numerous heads poised like a hood above his crown. There is deep significance attached to Vishnu's demeanor and to the serpent. Vishnu represents pure consciousness. The numerous serpent heads represent the mind cluttered with thoughts, but the serpent is not moving. The thoughts of the mind are subdued.

Vishnu is blue, to indicate all-pervasiveness and the infinite. It is the color attributed to the sky and endless space and to the ocean, where the depth is usually beyond our vision. The sky symbolically connects us between the

FIGURE 54

Vishnu

world of gods and the earthly world, with blue associated with the sacred. Vishnu moves between these two worlds, moves between the unseen and the seen. The crown on Vishnu's head reflects his supreme rule, and in this capacity Vishnu is the protector and the preserver of the universe.

Each of Vishnu's four hands carries an object. The sacred lotus is the Truth and Vishnu holds it to remind us to reach within ourselves to aim for this final goal. A conch shell spreads the primordial word—AUM—and reminds us of the noble goals of life that are related to the dharma and the inner self. A discus or *chakra* (wheel) represents the cycle of time, which we strive to break through moksha or liberation. Vishnu also carries a mace which he uses to help lift up the fallen and to knock down the evil forces within us that steer us from the right path.

Vishnu has nine avatars (manifestations) that he sent to earth to defeat evil and protect the law of dharma at various times during the earth's existence. The avatars are an expression of the cycle of evolution and the evolution within man that must take place to realize moksha. The first avatar was a fish, the seventh was Rama, the eighth was Krishna, and the ninth avatar was the Buddha, who spread the principle of non-violence. A tenth avatar is yet to come.

Vishnu is often depicted with his consort, Lakshmi, the goddess of wealth. His vehicle is the *garuda*, which is half man and half bird. The garuda, which spreads Vedic knowledge, flies with great speed and strength that enables it to reach great heights—symbolizing the transcendence above earthly barriers.

Lakshmi

Lakshmi, the consort of Vishnu, is the goddess of wealth. But wealth includes an abundance of proper values and spiritual goodness that should be cultivated by each worshipper. With each avatar of Vishnu, Lakshmi assumes a different role and name; however, she always represents the Shakti or power that is represented in each avatar.

As the popular and beautiful Goddess Lakshmi, it is her wealth (in the broad definition of wealth) that helps Vishnu in his role as the preserver. Lakshmi usually stands or sits on a lotus, the symbol of the Truth that should by gained by mankind. The concept of knowledge is also reflected in the notion of wealth. To acquire wealth, we need to acquire knowledge. When Lakshmi's hand is pointed down, this symbolizes the gesture of giving. Typically, an image of Lakshmi is found in every Hindu home and commercial establishment.

FIGURE 55

Lakshmi

FIGURE 56

Rama

Rama

Rama, whose story is told in the *Ramayana*—the great Hindu epic—is the seventh avatar of Vishnu. In the evolution toward self-realization, Rama represents the importance of detachment from earthly desires. Sent to earth as the son of a king, Rama's duty was to destroy the evil embodied in Ravana, a powerful rival king. His mission required him to go into the forest to rescue his wife, Sita. Then, once he saved Sita from evil, Rama had to send her into exile. Throughout his mission on earth, however, Rama served as the symbol of goodness. He never wavered from his dharma and was the example of the perfect son, brother, husband, father, friend, and leader.

To Hindus, Rama represents the embodiment of the ideal man. He is adorned in royal garments and usually wears a crown and a string of jewels that remind us of his perfect attributes. Rama also carries a bow with arrows so that he is ready to conquer any challenges within himself and the external world in order to fulfill his dharma. The bow and arrow also reflect Rama's intense strength and the power that enables him to remain spiritually and morally strong.

Krishna

After Rama, Vishnu sent the seed of Krishna to earth when the world was suffering from horrific disasters created by more demonic kings. The actions of these kings represent the negative qualities that prevent enlightenment. Krishna, whose body is blue, was born at night inside a prison. His name in Sanskrit means dark, and he represents the emergence of truth and spiritual enlightenment in the limiting realm of darkness. Krishna, the next stage toward self-realization, is the realization of Truth, and represents the state of bliss.

As a young boy, Krishna was energetic—a dynamic representation of the power of Vishnu. Repeatedly, he teased young *gopis* (milkmaids)—symbols of desire and distraction—and charmed them with the music of his flute, which represents the ecstasy that comes with self-realization. Krishna is often depicted with one foot gently crossed over the other ankle in a pose of contentment. Ultimately, his behavior reveals the joy that comes with the realization of the Truth.

FIGURE 57

Krishna

Hanuman

Hanuman is the monkey god who represents wisdom, strength, and devotion to dharma. He willingly comes to the aid of those who sincerely worship him. When Rama asked Hanuman to find medicinal herbs in the Himalayas, the monkey god flew off and brought back an entire mountain peak. Hanuman couldn't recognize the medicinal herb, yet he was determined to do his duty. Hanuman usually carries a huge mace or club to destroy evil. One hand is often held palm upward, which signifies spiritual blessings.

FIGURE 58

Hanuman

SYMBOLIC REPRESENTATIONS

You can also select discreet, symbolic representations of these deities for your vastu living space. Here are some suggestions, but you can choose anything that relates to the specific attributes that are associated with each deity. Refer back to their descriptions above.

Deity	Symbolic Representation
Brahma	lotus, carving or picture of swan, string of beads
Saraswati	old book, sheet of music, lotus, carving or picture of peacock or swan
Shiva	polished oval stone to represent Shiva's Linga, carving or picture of a bull
Parvati	gold-colored beads, lotus
Durga	carving or picture of tiger or lion
Ganesha	carving or picture of an elephant
Vishnu	conch shell, carving or picture of one of his avatars, such as the fish, the tortoise, the Buddha.
Lakshmi	collection of coins
Rama	bow and arrow
Krishna	wooden flute
Hanuman	carving or picture of a monkey

Finally, please understand that you can choose a deity from your own religion, a symbol that is identified with your religion, something from nature, which is also divine, or an appropriate daytime color, provided they represent similar qualities to the Vedic deities. All that is required is the sincerity behind your appeasement and your acceptance of the Vedic theories that support vastu:

1. an undeniable order and harmony exists in the universe;
2. everything that exists is animated;
3. all existence is interconnected;
4. the essence of everything is part of That—the supreme creative force or Tat Tvam Asi, which is Sanskrit for Thou Art That.

If you can accept this view of the world, whatever appeasements you choose will act as powerful olive branches, keeping the elements and deities in harmony. So let vastu living into your life—let it encircle you with its spiritual strength. No matter how much time you spend creating the best possible alignment of the elements in your home and workspace, you will reap positive rewards. Peace will prevail. Inner peace will prevail. You will have created a home for your soul.

APPENDICES

Appendix I

THE RAGA AND VASTU

"Architecture in general is frozen music." This analogy, made by German philosopher Frederick Von Schelling (1775–1854) is so accurate when we consider the classical Indian music called the raga and great Indian architecture, such as the temple described in Khajuraho (see Chapter 3, *Vastu in Ancient Temple Design*). The similarities between the two disciplines extend beyond an artistic relationship. As with vastu, the raga has a Vedic philosophical and spiritual foundation that moves the music well beyond the realm of art.

Other links between vastu and the raga are there to be seen and heard. The names of ragas evoke three-dimensional images that are then expressed through the music. The raga understands the power of color and evokes color through its notes and melodies. And just as a particular color brings a certain set of feelings to a vastu room or a vastu building, color expressed through a note or melody brings its intended set of feelings to the raga.

THE RAGA AND ITS MUSICAL ELEMENTS

The raga adheres to a system that is very different from Western music. Indeed, it is difficult to describe a raga by using the terminology attached to our music. The application of the two words—notes and rhythm— to the

217

raga is imprecise. The two words are too limiting. The raga speaks of *swara* and *tala*. Swara, a Sanskrit word, means more than a note; it has a spiritual and philosophical subtext that means literally "the self bursting forth." Tala, which is also a specific measurement used historically in vastu, represents the raga's cycle of beats, rhythmic structure, meter, cadence—-any number of phrases that add more meaning to the Western concept of rhythm. The tala is associated with mantras and the poetic cadence in the verbal expression of the Vedic hymns, so tala is also a word with deep spiritual associations. As for raga, this word is variously defined as a melodic concept, a melodic structure, a melodic pattern based around a scale of specific notes.

PARALLELS WITH VASTU

CONCEPT OF RHYTHM AND OBJECTIVE

Two strong parallels bind the raga to vastu: the concept of rhythm as its relates to the creation of a specific mood, and the primary objective of the raga, which is so similar to the objective in vastu. A raga is therapeutic. It is meant to uplift and transform the soul—the soul of the artist and the soul of each listener. And this objective is not just a casual by-product of the raga, any more than it is a casual by-product of vastu. This spiritual objective is the driving force behind each discipline and art form.

THE POWER OF AUM

The same connection between music and architecture also relates to sound and AUM, the first word uttered by Lord Brahma, the primordial word that set creation in motion. The *Vedas* were heard by rishis, who chanted the sacred words for an unknown period of time until they were finally codified and provided with their present meter. Indian classical music, especially the raga, illustrates the power of vibration and reflects the profound meanings attached to AUM, the purest of energy, which is behind the cycle of creation, preservation, and destruction—the force that keeps creation in motion.

As a result, ragas are more than vibrations that become music to the ears. Ragas evoke the sacredness of AUM and are designed to draw out the connection that exists between the self and the Supreme Creative Force. The raga and vastu are both related to the power of vibration and its effect on the human body, mind, and soul. The two disciplines are connected to our spiritual growth and enlightenment. Vastu and the raga are deeply connected to rhythm—not just in structure, but in the expression of the importance of the cycle of time.

THE IMPORTANCE OF NATURE

As with vastu, the raga consciously connects to nature. The raga expresses the Vedic holistic belief through subject and sound. Each raga was created for a clearly defined time of day, time of season, type of weather. When a student learns the raga, he or she must meditate deeply on the associations connected to this specific time or season so that the correct moods are evoked through the notes linked to the raga. Particular notes define the cycle of time and season. The artist builds around the notes that dominate the raga and uses artistic, emotional, and spiritual expression to pass on to the listener the right feelings and thoughts that should be associated with this time of day or year.

When we hear the music, we are conscious of its connection to the cycle of time and the quality of nature. These characteristics are expressed through the structure, and this gives every raga its own personality—a personality governed and identified by its specific mood. This is also true with vastu. The rhythm of a building, including its proportions, is an important aspect of its form. The building's rhythm helps give each vastu creation a distinct personality that is appropriate to its form and function. The vastu temple transports us into the realm of the gods. The vastu home speaks to our soul, our mind, our body.

THE EXISTENCE OF GUIDELINES

There are guidelines for the structure of the raga, such as the particular notes that are to be played, exclusively, and the emphasis attached to specific notes within these chosen notes. But these guidelines, as in vastu, are guidelines that anchor the music so that it will ultimately resonate properly and achieve its objective. The guidelines exist as useful boundaries that provide, within the enclosed space, tremendous latitude for artistic creativity and freedom. In fact, a raga, unless it has been recorded, never sounds the same a second time, even when the performance is by the same artist. This leads to the second reminder of the connection between the raga and the cycle of creation, preservation, and destruction. The raga exists in a time frame limited by the performance. It is created slowly, then builds, intensifies, evolves, and spins back on itself, until it finally concludes with the vibrating silence—a silence that is mandatory and concludes the expression of AUM.

INTERCONNECTEDNESS

A successful performance of a raga brings us so far inside the music that we nearly become one with the performer. Often people in the audience will mimic the artist's hand gestures or they spontaneously express a word of appreciation when their inner self has been deeply touched. Listeners voluntarily connect to the music and the performer. Faces in the audience are normally unusually serene. This interconnectedness is intentional and vital, as important as it is in vastu. It makes us, the listener, feel one with the essence of the music. The raga inspires and soothes the soul. We realize that our own vibrations are connected to the vibrations of the beautiful sound that flows around and through us.

FROM DISCIPLE TO PERFORMER

The guru (teacher)–disciple relationship is extraordinarily personal; where the disciple learns more than the mastery of a particular instrument, including the voice. Because each raga has a personality and mood, the disciple must meditate deeply on these dimensions to get inside the raga and discover its essence. It takes years, even decades, to arrive at this point and an equal amount of concentrated devotion and dedication.

The disciple who becomes a performer and then possibly a great performer, usually called a *pandit* or *ustad*, has matured and become so spiritually and musically attuned to the essence of the raga—its connection to the Divine—-that his or her face and body are a reflection of the raga's beauty. We witness the effect of the raga on the performer's inner self. Just as in vastu where the home should be a reflection of the self, the maestro of the raga presents the self through the music. This is what is so unique about the concept of swara—-and why a raga is not just a collection of notes that we hear.

By the time the disciple becomes a performer, the structure of the music and the mood that it releases has caused a personal transformation. The artist is not using his or her body to annunciate the music; the music is using the artist as the messenger. The raga is in control; and the objective of the music is to make us, the listener, aware of its essence. The raga becomes a powerful spiritual tool that helps us along the path to enlightenment.

UNIVERSAL APPEAL

The raga is so carefully constructed through guidelines, which still allow tremendous artistic freedom, that we don't need to understand the words of the vocalist (if there is a vocalist) to be able to receive the message of the Truth contained within the raga. The spirit of the music sweeps through us as we listen; we surrender to it and let it inside our inner self. The raga's unusual power deserves to be heard, and this is the reason for listing the names of a few of the great Indian pandits and ustads who are masters of their particular instrument and the presentation of the raga. Unfortunately, a couple of these great artists are now deceased, but you can still hear them on CDs or tapes. And if you have an opportunity to see the others perform in a concert, try to attend. The experience will be memorable and haunting—even if you know nothing more about the raga than this brief introduction.

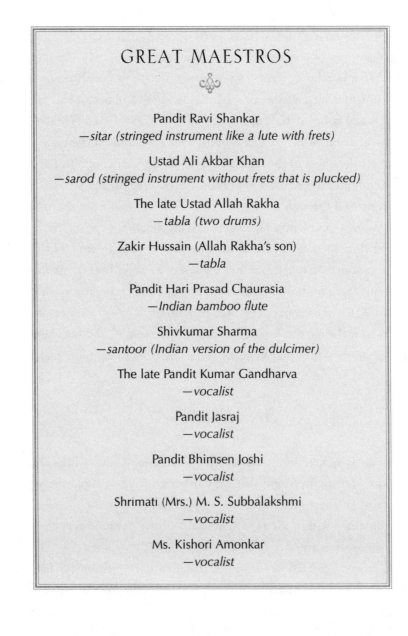

GREAT MAESTROS

Pandit Ravi Shankar
—*sitar (stringed instrument like a lute with frets)*

Ustad Ali Akbar Khan
—*sarod (stringed instrument without frets that is plucked)*

The late Ustad Allah Rakha
—*tabla (two drums)*

Zakir Hussain (Allah Rakha's son)
—*tabla*

Pandit Hari Prasad Chaurasia
—*Indian bamboo flute*

Shivkumar Sharma
—*santoor (Indian version of the dulcimer)*

The late Pandit Kumar Gandharva
—*vocalist*

Pandit Jasraj
—*vocalist*

Pandit Bhimsen Joshi
—*vocalist*

Shrimati (Mrs.) M. S. Subbalakshmi
—*vocalist*

Ms. Kishori Amonkar
—*vocalist*

APPENDIX II

HARMONY THROUGH DIET

Creating a home for the soul through vastu is such a healthy decision. But why not supplement vastu by reviewing the following dietary guidelines so that your body can also reflect a state of balance and harmony? Too often, we tend to eat what our mind craves. We forget that our food choices should really be based on what is good for our body—our muscles, our bones, our organs, every single cell. Far too often we ignore our body's own signals and commit forms of self-sabotage that decrease the health of our body, mind, and soul. This unfortunate habit also diminishes the positive benefits of vastu. So please remember: we really are what we eat.

LISTENING TO YOUR BODY

VATA

If you discovered through the questionnaire in Chapter 5, *Getting Started*, that you appear to have a vata (air)-dominant constitution, you probably tend to suffer from these health problems when your vata is off-balance:

Arthritis and stiff joints   Constipation

Insomnia and fatigue   Cracked nails

Flatulence   Dry skin

PITTA

If you discovered through the questionnaire that you appear to have a pitta (fire) dominant constitution, you probably tend to suffer from these health problems when your pitta is off-balance:

Hyperacidity   Ulcers

Liver and gall bladder disorders   Skin rashes

Colitis

KAPHA

If you discovered through the questionnaire that you appear to have a kapha (water)–dominant constitution, you probably tend to suffer from these health problems when your kapha is off-balance:

Coughs and colds   Respiratory problems

Bronchitis   Sinusitis

Asthma   Obesity

THERAPEUTIC DIETS

An appropriate diet—one that matches our constitution—can help us keep our constitution or dosha, as it called in Sanskrit, in balance. The main rule to remember is that like increases like. So when you plan to eat, consider the following seasonal guidelines, which are appropriate for all doshas, and the general guidelines that are specific to each dosha.

GENERAL DIETARY RULES

Seasonal

- When the weather is summery hot, lower your intake of warm foods and hot beverages. Cold food is best.
- When the weather is wintry cold, eat less cold foods and cold beverages and focus on hot meals for nourishment.
- During windy dry weather, try not to have too many vata foods (see below). Vata foods aggravate the body's tendency to respond in kind to these conditions. The skin and joints can lose their natural lubrication.

GENERAL RULES FOR EACH DOSHA

VATA	PITTA	KAPHA
Eat warm cooked foods that are a bit heavy and oily.	Eat cool foods that contain lots of liquids.	Eat warm foods that are light and dry.
Eat cooked and watery vegetables; avoid too many salads and raw vegetables.	Choose vegetables that are sweet or bitter; avoid pungent vegetables.	Eat some raw vegetables and vegetables that are pungent and bitter; avoid sweet and watery vegetables.
Avoid too many beans; choose soy products, such as tofu.	Eat a moderate amount of beans and soy products, such as tofu.	Can eat most beans, but avoid soy products.

VATA	PITTA	KAPHA
Choose sweet and sour fruits; avoid dry crunchy fruit.	Choose sweet fruits; avoid sour fruits.	Choose astringent fruit; avoid sweet and sour fruit.
Avoid red meat.	Try to be vegetarian; avoid red meat and seafood.	Limit intake of red meat.
Eat all dairy products, in moderation.	Stick to milk and butter.	Avoid too much dairy; drink only low-fat milk.
Eat nuts, in moderation.	Stick to sunflower seeds or a moderate amount of almonds.	Try to avoid eating nuts.
Good tolerance for most oils.	See list for appropriate oils.	Use oil in moderation.
Don't have too many hot spices.	Concentrate on cool spices, such as cilantro, coriander, cinnamon, dill, fennel, basil, cardamom.	Most spices are good except salt.

KEEPING YOUR DOSHA IN BALANCE

Here are some specific foods to enjoy or avoid that have a particular effect on your constitution. Try to eat a healthy amount of the food in the "balances" list to help keep your dosha in balance. Conversely, when your body tells you that your dosha is aggravated, try to stay away from the foods in the "aggravates" list. Please remember, however, that these are dietary guidelines. For a personal evaluation and diet, contact an ayurveda practitioner. The books listed in the bibliography are also excellent introductions to ayurveda and provide good guidance.

	VATA		PITTA		KAPHA	
Food Category	Balances	Aggravates	Balances	Aggravates	Balances	Aggravates
GRAINS	White rice	Millet	White rice	Corn	Millet	Too much wheat
	Brown rice	Corn	Barley	Rye	Barley	Too much rice
	Wheat		Wheat			
			Oats			
VEGETABLES	Beets	Cabbage	Asparagus	Hot peppers	Beets	Zucchini
	Carrots	Cauliflower	Broccoli	Tomatoes	Broccoli	Cucumber
	Green beans	Broccoli	Cabbage	Spinach	Cabbage	Tomatoes
	Zucchini	Brussels sprouts	Cauliflower	Radishes	Carrots	Sweet potatoes
	Asparagus		Celery	Carrots	Cauliflower	
	Sweet potatoes		Cucumber		Celery	
			Okra		Eggplant	
			Peas		Leafy greens	
			Sweet potatoes		Mushrooms	
			Sweet peppers		Okra	
			Zucchini		Onions	
			Green Beans		White potatoes	

227

Food Category	VATA		PITTA		KAPHA	
	Balances	Aggravates	Balances	Aggravates	Balances	Aggravates
VEGETABLES			Leafy greens		Radishes	
					Spinach	
					Brussels sprouts	
					Parsley	
					Peas	
					Asparagus	
FRUITS	Grapes	Apples	Avocados	Tangy oranges	Apples	Cantaloupe
	Bananas	Cranberries	Coconuts	Apricots	Berries	Watermelon
	Cherries	Dried fruit	Figs	Cranberries	Cherries	Grapes
	Papayas		Red grapes	Lemons	Cranberries	Grapefruit
	Avocados		Sweet melons	Green grapes	Pomegranates	Lemons
	Berries		Sweet oranges	Grapefruit	Pears	Tangy oranges
	Mangoes		Plums		Apricots	Bananas
	Sweet oranges		Pomegranates			
			Pineapples			

Food Category	VATA		PITTA		KAPHA	
	Balances	Aggravates	Balances	Aggravates	Balances	Aggravates
FRUITS			Pears Prunes Apples			
ANIMAL PRODUCTS	White chicken White turkey Seafood Eggs	Beef Pork Lamb	White chicken White turkey	Beef Seafood Egg yolk	White chicken White turkey Seafood	Too much beef Too much pork Too much lamb
OILS	Olive Sesame		Sunflower Olive Canola		Corn Sunflower	
SWEETENERS	Best choices: Honey Maple syrup Molasses		Can use all sweeteners except: Honey Molasses		Avoid sweeteners except for honey	

229

GLOSSARY

acharya	highly respected teacher
amrit	the nectar that brings *moksha* or liberation from the cycle of rebirth
angula	measurement based on the thickness of the first joint of the adult middle finger
antarala	vestibule of the temple
atma	soul or essence
avatars	manifestations
ayurveda	science of life
Brahmasthana	the place of God, the name for the sacred center of a vastu space
chakra	wheel
chanda	rhythm and order
chinmudra	a hand gesture where the index finger is bent down to the thumb to create a zero. The zero reminds us to bend our ego and reduce it to zero.
dharma	duty—the duty to adhere to right principles as prescribed in the Vedic texts
dhoti	long wrap worn around the lower half of a man's body
dhurrie	woven rug of cotton or wool or camel hair
dosha	an ayurveda term that relates to the elements of fire, water, and air and their balance or imbalance within the body

garbhagriha	womb chamber, another word for the inner sanctum
garuda	a creature that is half man and half bird
gopis	milkmaids
jagati	temple platform or terrace
jyotish	Indian astrology
kalasha	the vessel on top of the temple that symbolically holds the nectar of immortality
kapha	a dosha in the body's physical constitution that is related primarily to the element of water
kurta	long flowing shirt
kilim	a woven tapestry rug
linga	phallus and symbol of Shiva
maha-mandapa	enclosed hall of a temple
mahatma	great soul
mandala	spiritual geometric diagram or grid
mandapa	initial compartment of the temple
mantra	sacred formula expressed as a chant
marmas	vulnerable points in the vastu purusha
moksha	liberation from the cycle of rebirth
mudra	symbolic hand gesture
mukha-mandapa	entrance porch of a temple
namaste	hands held together at the chest; symbolic Hindu gesture used to greet or say goodbye to someone. Most popular meaning: "I bow to the divine within you"
pada	form of measurement equivalent to the size of a man's foot
pandit	Hindu scholar or master
Paramaatma	Supreme Soul or essence of the Supreme Creator or Divine Force
pitta	a dosha in the body's physical constitution that is related to the element of fire
prakriti	visible matter
prana	life force or energy within the body

231

puja	prayer service
Puranas	ancient stories
purusha	soul, unseen essence, divine being
raga	Indian classical music; a raga is a melodic concept, a melodic structure, a melodic pattern based around a scale of notes
rishi	seer
rupee	Indian currency
Sanatana Dharma	eternal faith, the original name of Hinduism
sastras	treatise or text
Shakti	female power or active energy
swara	literally "self bursting forth"; the notes in Indian classical music, such as the raga
swastika	Vedic symbol of well-being and auspiciousness that was cynically corrupted by Hitler
tala	form of measurement equivalent to the size of a typical human palm or face; tala is also the cycle of beats, the rhythmic structure, the meter, the cadence in Indian classical music, such as the raga
Tat Tvam Asi	Sanskrit for "Thou Art That"
toran	an Indian banner hung over a door that showers blessings on all who walk underneath it
tikka	symbolic mark placed on the center of the forehead to represent the third eye associated with wisdom
Upanisads	the concluding wisdom and philosophy that ends the sacred *Vedas*
ustad	maestro used traditionally for Moslems
vastu	land or site, or any built form, including the human form
vastu purusha	cosmic spirit of the land or site
vata	a dosha in the body's physical constitution that is related to the element of air

Vedas	spiritual texts that form the backbone of Hinduism
vina	stringed instrument
yoga	to unite—a series of practices that lead one to the realization of the self
yugas	divisions of time allocated to the lifespan of the universe

BIBLIOGRAPHY

THE *VEDAS*, VEDIC CULTURE, AND HINDUISM

The *Upanisads* in separate volumes, with translation and commentaries by Swami Chinmayananda (Pennsylvania: Chinmaya Publications, Chinmaya Mission West Publications Division).

The *Holy Geeta (Bhagavad Gita)*, with translation and commentary by Swami Chinmayananda (Pennsylvania: Chinmaya Publications, Chinmaya Mission West Publications Division).

The Vedas by Sri Chandrasekharendra Sawaswati (Mumbai: Bharatiya Vidya Bhavan, Sudakshina Trust, 1998).

Sadhana: The Realization of Life by Rabindranath Tagore (Chennai: Macmillan India, 1988).

Gods, Sages and Kings by David Frawley (Salt Lake City: Passage Press, 1991).

Art of God Symbolism by Swami Chinmayananda (Pennsylvania: Chinmaya Publications, Chinmaya Mission West Publications Division).

Hindu Culture: An Introduction, transcription of lectures by Swami Tejomayananda (Pennsylvania: Chinmaya Publications, Chinmaya Mission West Publications Division, 1994).

VASTU

Manasara Series, 7 Volumes, Prasanna Kumar Acharya, ed. and trans. (New Delhi: Munshiram Manoharlal Publishers, 1934).

Mayamata, 2 Volumes, Kapila Vatsyayan, general ed. and Bruno Dagens, trans. (Delhi: Indira Gandhi National Centre for the Arts in association with Motilal Banarsidass Publishers, 1994).

Vastu Sastra, Hindu Science of Architecture, 2 Volumes by D. N. Shukla (Delhi: Munshiram Manoharlal Publishers, 1993).

THE HINDU TEMPLE

Hindu Temple, 2 Volumes by Stella Kramrisch (New Delhi: Motilal Banarsidass Publishers, 1995).

Khajuraho by Krishna Deva (Delhi: Brijbasi Printers, 1991).

The Religious Imagery of Khajuraho by Devangana Desai (Mumbai: Franco-Indian Research, Pvt. Ltd., 1996).

YOGA

The Tree of Yoga by B.K.S. Iyengar and Daniel Rivers-Moore, ed. (New Delhi: HarperCollins Publishers India, 1988).

Yoga: The Ultimate Attainment by Swami Rajarshi Muni (New Delhi, Jaico Publishing House, 1995).

AYURVEDA

Ayurveda & Panchakarma by Sunil V. Joshi M.D., (Ayu) (Delhi: Motilal Banarsidass Publishers, 1998).

Ayurveda The Science of Self-Healing by Dr. Vasant Lad (Wisconsin: Lotus Light, 1990).

Natural Healing Through Ayurveda by Professor Dr. Subash Ranade (Delhi: Motilal Banarsidass Publishers, 1994).

Ayurveda: The Ancient Indian Healing Art by Scott Gerson, Md. (New York: Barnes and Noble by arrangement with Element Books Limited, 1997).

The Ayurveda Encyclopedia by Swami Sada Shiva Tirtha (New York, Ayurveda Holistic Center Press, 1998).

The books on ayurveda by Deepak Chopra, such as *Perfect Digestion* and *Boundless Energy* (New York: Three Rivers Press, 1997).

INDIAN FOOD

Indian Food: A Historical Companion by K.T. Achaya (Delhi: Oxford University Press, 1998).

VASTU LIVING:
QUICK REFERENCE CHART

If you live in the southern hemisphere, do remember to rotate the element and deity 90 degrees to the right.

Direction	Element	Deity	About The Zone
Northeast	Water	Isa	The northeast, the gateway to the gods, is the recipient of positive cosmic energy. This quadrant should not have heavy or tall objects so that the energy can move freely through the space. The element of water reinforces calm and tranquility.
Southeast	Fire	Agni	The southeast belongs to the element of fire, which brings heat and passion. Agni symbolizes the sacred fire and so this quadrant acts as a great purifier.
Southwest	Earth	Pitri	The southwest quadrant, which is the realm of the earth element, should be built up and reinforced with heavier objects that hold in the cosmic energy. This quadrant is associated with strength. As the region of Pitri, the lord of ancestors, the southwest also embodies the wisdom of the departed.
Northwest	Air	Vayu	The northwest, representing the element of air, signifies movement and restlessness. The wind comes and goes. The northwest is also an area that brings a quick flow of ideas.

Center	Space	Brahma	Spiritual power radiates out from the center, which is the realm of the element of space and the location of Brahma, the creator. It is the inner sanctum of the home or workspace and provides spiritual well-being and the important connection to the Supreme Creator.
North		Kuber	The lord of wealth and indulgence blesses us with abundance—not limited to financial abundance but extended to spiritual abundance.
		Soma	The lord of the moon and health provides light in darkness, protects our health and restores our energy while we sleep.
East		Surya	The lord of the sun, who brings light to each day, gives us enlightenment and inspiration.
South		Yama	The lord of death also judges our performance of dharma (duty and responsibility). Yama serves as a reminder for restraint to those who are tempted by his cardinal opposite, Lord Kama.
West		Varuna	The lord of the oceans, the unknown, and darkness, Varuna ushers in the night and welcomes the appearance of celestial light.

1. The north and the east should bear less weight than the south and the west.

2. The north and the east should be less built-up than the south and the west.

3. A slope in a property should extend down the north, the northeast, or the east, and this area should not have any tall or heavy obstacles that repel the positive cosmic energies.

4. The elevated portion of a property should be in the south, the southwest, or the west. These same areas should have heavy objects that can keep the energy inside the property, dwelling, or workspace.

5. Heavy furniture should be in the south and the west; lighter furniture should be in the north and the east.

6. Respect the sacred center by keeping it empty. This allows you to receive the gift of spiritual well-being.

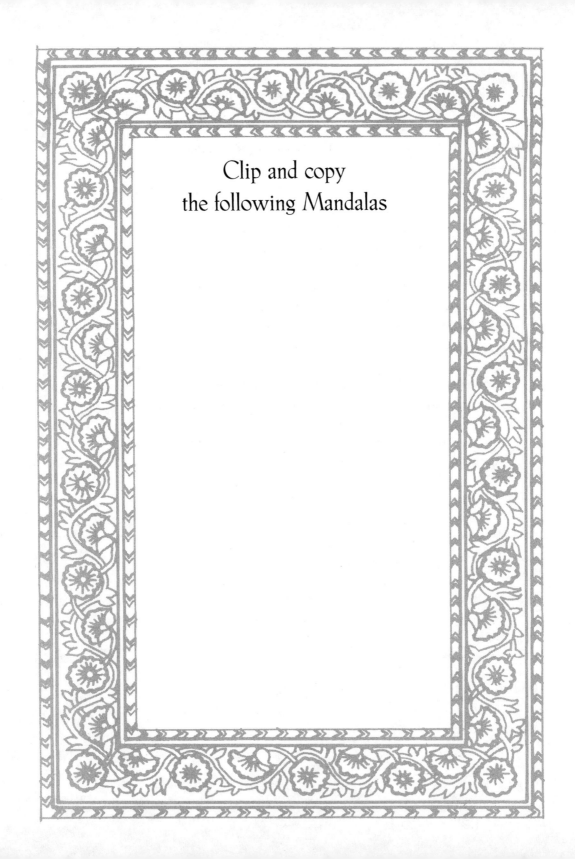

Clip and copy
the following Mandalas

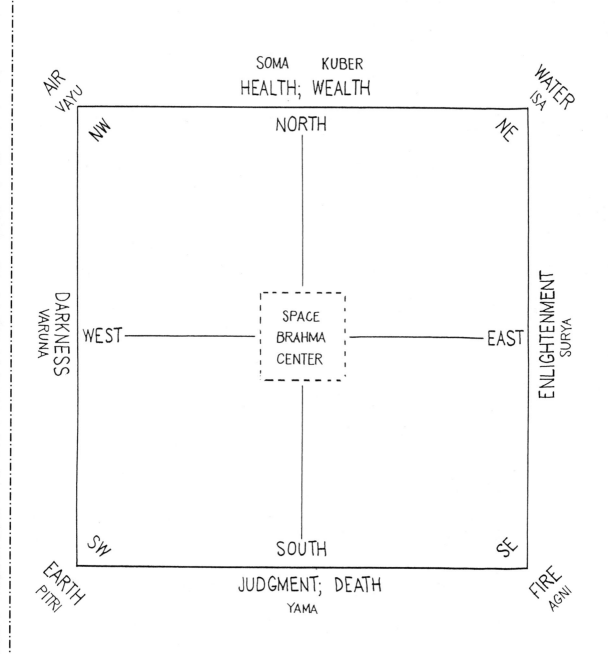

Vastu Purusha Mandala Square

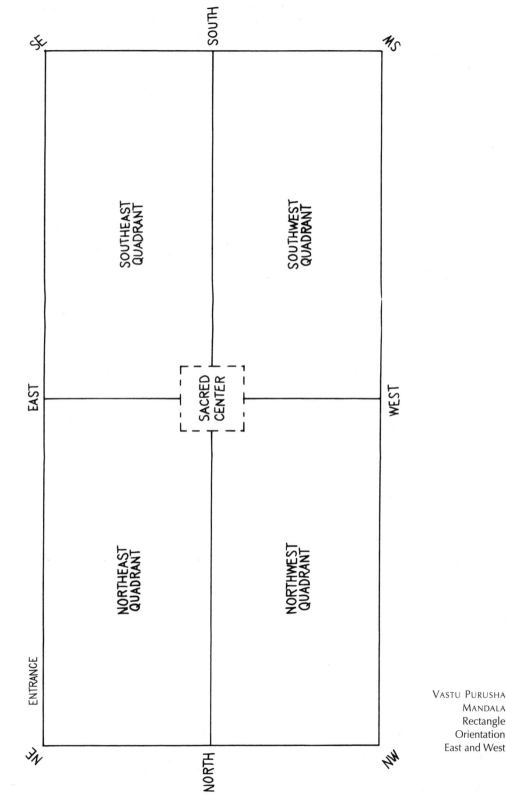

SOUTH

SE

WS

SOUTHEAST
QUADRANT

SOUTHWEST
QUADRANT

EAST

SACRED
CENTER

WEST

NORTHEAST
QUADRANT

NORTHWEST
QUADRANT

ENTRANCE

NE

NW

NORTH

Vastu Purusha
Mandala
Rectangle
Orientation
East and West

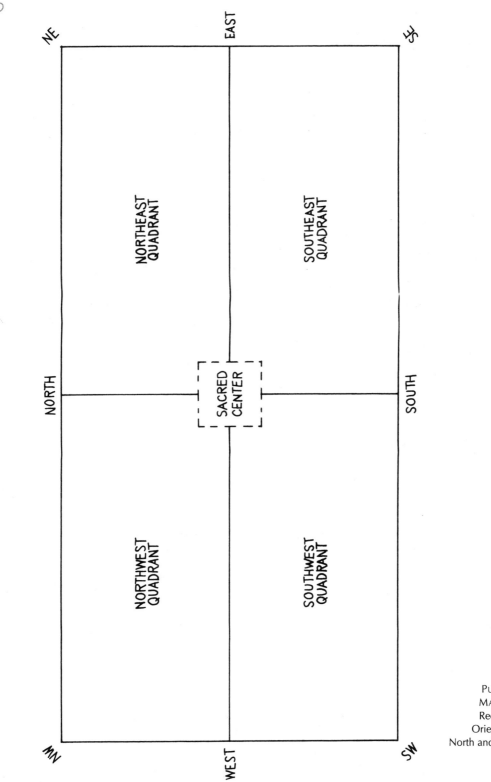

NORTHEAST QUADRANT

SOUTHEAST QUADRANT

NORTHWEST QUADRANT

SOUTHWEST QUADRANT

SACRED CENTER

NE

EAST

SE

NORTH

SOUTH

NW

WEST

SW

VASTU
PURUSHA
MANDALA
Rectangle
Orientation
North and South

⚜

ABOUT THE AUTHOR

KATHLEEN COX, a journalist who first visited India in 1985, lived in New Delhi throughout the 1990s. She has traveled throughout the subcontinent and has served as a consultant for the private sector and the Government of India. She has been researching Vedic traditions for the past decade; she started her formal vastu education in 1997 and studied with a prominent Indian architect and vastu scholars. Cox has written extensively about India's culture and business development for major publications in the United States and India, including the *Wall Street Journal*, the *Los Angeles Times*, *Travel and Leisure* (Asian Edition), *Harper's Bazaar*, and the *Times of India*. She was the principal contributor to many successive editions of Fodor's *India* and is the author of Fodor's *The Himalayan Countries*. She lives in New York City, where she consults and lectures on vastu living. She can be reached via her web site, www.vastuliving.com.

ABOUT THE ILLUSTRATOR

ALLISON EDEN KARN received her Bachelor of Arts and Master of Architecture from Yale University. When she is not drawing Hindu deities or vastu-compliant furnishings, she is busy at work in New York City designing architecture and interiors.

247